D0984636

THE LEISURE CLASS
IN AMERICA

THE LEISURE CLASS
IN AMERICA

Advisory Editor
Leon Stein

A Note About This Volume

One of a number of would-be successors to Ward McAllister as society's dictator, Nichols compiled his own list of top social leaders and outstanding families. The chief value of his compendium, however, is in the seven essays that accompanied his list. These comprise a kind of Machiavellian guide to the achievement of high rank and the means by which superior position may be defended against all challengers.

See last pages of this volume for a complete list of titles.

THE

ULTRA-FASHIONABLE

PEERAGE OF AMERICA

BY

CHARLES WILBUR de LYON NICHOLS

ARNO PRESS

A New York Times Company

New York / 1975

Reprint Edition 1975 by Arno Press Inc.

THE LEISURE CLASS IN AMERICA
ISBN for complete set: 0-405-06900-6
See last pages of this volume for titles.

Manufactured in the United States of America

———••◦∞◦••———

Library of Congress Cataloging in Publication Data

Nicholls, Charles Wilbur de Lyon, 1854-1923.
    The ultra-fashionable peerage of America.

    (The Leisure class in America)
    Reprint of the ed. published by G. Harjes, New York.
    1. United States--Social life and customs--1865-1918.
2. United States--Social registers. I. Title.
II. Title: Peerage of America. III. Series.
E168.N63 1975   920'.073   75-1864
ISBN 0-405-06930-8

THE

ULTRA-FASHIONABLE

PEERAGE OF AMERICA

C. W. de Lyon Nichols

THE

ULTRA-FASHIONABLE

PEERAGE OF AMERICA

AN OFFICIAL LIST

OF THOSE PEOPLE WHO CAN PROPERLY BE CALLED

ULTRA-FASHIONABLE

IN THE UNITED STATES.

WITH A FEW APPENDED ESSAYS ON

ULTRA-SMARTNESS

BY

CHARLES WILBUR DE LYON NICHOLS

AUTHOR OF

"The Greek Madonna," "The Décadents," "The Sunday
Kindergarten Art History Catechism," etc.

NEW YORK

GEORGE HARJES, PUBLISHER

1904

PREFACE.

❧ ❧ ❧

*T*HE gentle or irate reader of these pages is fore-warned not to expect from them a genealogic-al treatise. The subject in hand—National Society, is treated wholly from the standpoint of fashion; birth and hereditary rank, being accounted mere accidents and not belonging to the essence of smartness. Furthermore, the system of distinctions employed in the Ultra-fashionable Peerage of America, sweeps away as so much social under-crust more than ninety per cent. of the oldest families of the Republic. On the other hand, a truly American spirit pervading the work, evinces itself in the large measure of influence it assigns to the social talent of the individual as one of the main factors in insuring the highest social success.

As Burke's Peerage is diversified by five different grades of nobility, so in the Ultra-fashionable Peerage of America, five descending degrees of fashionable precedence obtain: 1st, the Ultra-smart "150"; 2nd, the "400," supplemented by a limited few Ultra-fashionable folk of the provincial cities and towns; 3d, the outer fringe of the "400"; 4th, the Colonial and Knickerbocker families; 5th, the wealthy upper middle class in American society—society in the crude.

THE AUTHOR.

CONTENTS.

The Ultra-fashionable Peerage of America.

THE 150

MRS. ASTOR

VICEREGAL LEADERS OF THE 150.

MRS. OGDEN MILLS

MRS. CORNELIUS VANDERBILT, JR.

MRS. JOHN JACOB ASTOR

MRS. OGDEN GOELET

THE 150

1 - 2   COL. AND MRS. JOHN JACOB ASTOR

3 - 4   MR. AND MRS. EDMUND L. BAYLIES

5 - 6   MR. AND MRS. TOWNSEND BURDEN

7 - 8   THE MISSES BURDEN

9 - 10   MR. AND MRS. WILLIAM A. M. BURDEN

11   MR. TOWNSEND BURDEN, JR.

12 - 13   MR. AND MRS. JAMES A. BURDEN, JR.

14   MRS. BURKE-ROCHE

15   MISS CYNTHIA BURKE-ROCHE

16 - 17   MR. AND MRS. OLIVER H. P. BELMONT

18 - 19   MR. AND MRS. EDWARD J. BERWIND

20 - 21   MR. AND MRS. H. MORTIMER BROOKS

22 - 23   MR. AND MRS. REGINALD BROOKS

24 - 25	MR. AND MRS. ROYAL PHELPS CARROLL
26 - 27	MR. AND MRS. ROBERT J. COLLIER
28	MR. JAMES DE WOLFE CUTTING
29 - 30	MR. AND MRS. HENRY CLEWS
31 - 32	MR. AND MRS. ELISHA DYER, JR.
33 - 34	MR. AND MRS. GEORGE B. DE FOREST
35 - 36	MR. AND MRS. JOHN R. DREXEL
37 - 38	MR. AND MRS. STUYVESANT FISH
39	MRS. OGDEN GOELET
40 - 41	MR. AND MRS. ROBERT GOELET *née* WHELEN
42	MRS. ROBERT GOELET
43	MR. ROBERT WALTON GOELET
44 - 45	MR. AND MRS. ELBRIDGE T. GERRY
46 - 47	THE MISSES GERRY
48	MR. ROBERT LIVINGSTON GERRY
49 - 50	MR. AND MRS. GEORGE JAY GOULD
51	MRS. RICHARD GAMBRILL
52 - 53	MR. AND MRS. CHARLES DANA GIBSON
54 - 55	MR. AND MRS. HARRY O. HAVEMEYER, JR.
56 - 57	MR. AND MRS. OLIVER HARRIMAN
58 - 59	MR. AND MRS. C. OLIVER ISELIN
60	MISS NORA ISELIN
61	MISS THÉRÈSE ISELIN
62 - 63	MR. AND MRS. ERNEST ISELIN
64 - 65	MR. AND MRS. PEMBROKE JONES
66 - 67	COLONEL AND MRS. WILLIAM JAY
68	MISS ELEANOR JAY
69	MR. WOODBURY KANE
70	MRS. JAMES P. KERNOCHAN
71 - 72	MR. AND MRS. HENRY SYMES LEHR
73 - 74	MR. AND MRS. PHILIP M. LYDIG

8

75 - 76	MR. AND MRS. LEVI P. MORTON
77	MISS MORTON
78 - 79	MR. AND MRS. E. ROLLINS MORSE
80 - 81	MR. AND MRS. W. STARR MILLER
82 - 83	MR. AND MRS. CLARENCE H. MACKAY
84 - 85	MR. AND MRS. OGDEN MILLS
86 - 87	THE MISSES MILLS
88	MR. OGDEN LIVINGSTON MILLS
89	MR. ALPHONSE DE NAVARRO
90	MRS. FREDERIC NEILSON
91 - 92	MR. AND MRS. HERMANN OELRICHS
93 - 94	MR. AND MRS. CHARLES M. OELRICHS
95	THE MARQUISE DE TALLEYRAND-PERIGORD
96	MR. JAMES V. PARKER
97 - 98	MR. AND MRS. REGINALD RIVES
99	MISS NATICA RIVES
100 - 101	MR. AND MRS. WHITELAW REID
102	MISS JEAN REID
103 - 104	MR. AND MRS. WINTHROP RUTHERFURD
105 - 106	MR. AND MRS. RUTHERFURD STUYVESANT
107	MISS LAURA PATTERSON SWAN
108	MR. LISPENARD STEWART
109 - 110	MR. AND MRS. WILLIAM DOUGLASS SLOANE
111	MR. JAMES HENRY SMITH
112 - 113	MR. AND MRS. SIDNEY J. SMITH
114 - 115	MR. AND MRS. HENRY A. C. TAYLOR
116 - 117	MR. AND MRS. H. McK. TWOMBLY
118	MR. THOMAS SUFFERN TAILER
119 - 120	MR. AND MRS. WILLIAM K. VANDERBILT
121 - 122	MR. AND MRS. WILLIAM K. VANDERBILT, JR.
123 - 124	MR. AND MRS. CORNELIUS VANDERBILT, JR.

125 - 126	MR. AND MRS. REGINALD VANDERBILT
127 - 128	MR. AND MRS. ALFRED G. VANDERBILT
129	MR. JAMES J. VAN ALEN
130	MISS VAN ALEN
131 - 132	MR. AND MRS. W. STORRS WELLS
133	MISS NATALIE WELLS
134 - 135	MR. AND MRS. RICHARD T. WILSON
136 - 137	MR. AND MRS. RICHARD T. WILSON, JR.
138 - 139	MR. AND MRS. ORME WILSON
140	MR. WORTHINGTON WHITEHOUSE
141 - 142	MR. AND MRS. WHITNEY WARREN
143	MISS CHARLOTTE WARREN
144 - 145	DR. AND MRS. W. SEWARD WEBB
146	MISS FREDERICKA WEBB
147 - 148	MR. AND MRS. HARRY PAYNE WHITNEY
149 - 150	MR. AND MRS. PAYNE WHITNEY

THE 400

MRS. ASTOR

1 - 2	MR. AND MRS. CHARLES B. ALEXANDER
3 - 4	MR. AND MRS. FREDERIC H. ALLEN
5	MR. L. F. HOLBROOK BETTS
6 - 7	MR. AND MRS. JAMES A. BURDEN, Sr.
8	MR. WILLIAMS P. BURDEN
9	MR. HENRY WORTHINGTON BULL
10 - 11	MR. AND MRS. CHARLES ASTOR BRISTED
12	MR. J. D. ROMAN BALDWIN
13	MISS LOUISE BALDWIN
14 - 15	MR. AND MRS. R. LIVINGSTON BEECKMAN
16	MRS. FREDERIC BRONSON
17	MISS ALICE BABCOCK
18	MR. EDWARD H. BULKLEY
19 - 20	MR. AND MRS. FREDERIC O. BEACH
21	MISS ANNA TOOKER BEST
22 - 23	MR. AND MRS. CHARLES T. BARNEY
24 - 25	MR. AND MRS. J. STEWART BARNEY
26	MISS HELEN T. BARNEY
27 - 28	MR. AND MRS. HENRI I. BARBEY
29	MISS BARBEY
30	MR. HENRY G. BARBEY
31	MR. ATHERTON BLIGHT
32 - 33	THE MISSES BLIGHT
34	MRS. HEBER R. BISHOP
35	MISS BISHOP

79	MR. WILLIAM B. CUTTING
80	MRS. MOSES TAYLOR CAMPBELL
81 - 82	MR. AND MRS. P. F. COLLIER
83	MISS CRYDER
84	MR. WILLIAM A. DUER
85	MISS CAROLINE KING DUER
86	MR. JOHN A. DIX
87	MISS MARGARET DIX
88 - 89	MR. AND MRS. CASIMIR DE RHAM
90 - 91	MR. AND MRS. BUTLER DUNCAN, JR.
92 - 93	MR. AND MRS. F. GRAND D'HAUTEVILLE
94	MR. PAUL GRAND D'HAUTEVILLE
95	MR. J. COLEMAN DRAYTON
96	MISS CAROLINE DRAYTON
97	MR. RALPH N. ELLIS
98 - 99	MR. AND MRS. H. LE ROY EMMET
100	MRS. HARGOUS-ELLIOT
101	MR. HENRY F. ELDRIDGE
102 - 103	MR. AND MRS. BLAIR FAIRCHILD
104 - 105	MR. AND MRS. E. G. FABBRI
106 - 107	MR. AND MRS. BRADHURST OSGOOD FIELD
108 - 109	MR. AND MRS. SETH BARTON FRENCH
110	MRS. FRANCIS ORMOND FRENCH
111 - 112	MR. AND MRS. THEODORE FRELINGHUYSEN
113 - 114	MR. AND MRS. CHARLES G. FRANCKLYN
115	MR. GORDON FELLOWS
116	MISS MARIAN FISH
117	MISS JANET FISH
118	MR. H. DE COURSEY FORBES
119 - 120	DR. AND MRS. AUSTIN FLINT, JR.
121 - 122	MR. AND MRS. JAMES W. GERARD, JR.

123 MR. JULIEN GERARD
124 MR. SUMNER GERARD
125 MR. F. GRAY GRISWOLD
126 - 127 MR. AND MRS. GOELET GALLATIN
128 MR. CENTER HITCHCOCK
129 MRS. THEODORE A. HAVEMEYER
130 - 131 MR. AND MRS. THEODORE A. HAVEMEYER, JR.
132 MR. FREDERICK C. HAVEMEYER
133 - 134 MR. AND MRS. FRANCIS BURTON HARRISON
135 - 136 MR. AND MRS. THOMAS HITCHCOCK
137 - 138 MR. AND MRS. THOMAS HITCHCOCK, JR.
139 - 140 MR. AND MRS. W. PIERSON HAMILTON
141 - 142 MR. AND MRS. THOMAS HASTINGS
143 - 144 MR. AND MRS. CHARLES F. HOFFMAN
145 MRS. SIBYL SHERMAN HOFFMAN
146 - 147 MR. AND MRS. FRANCIS BURRALL HOFFMAN
148 - 149 MR. AND MRS. JOHN H. HAMMOND
150 MISS MARION HAVEN
151 - 152 MR. AND MRS. GEO. GRISWOLD HAVEN, JR.
153 MR. GOOLD HOYT
154 MR. CYRIL HATCH
155 - 156 MR. AND MRS. E. HENRY HARRIMAN
157 - 158 THE MISSES MARY AND CORNELIA HARRIMAN
159 - 160 MR. AND MRS. J. BORDEN HARRIMAN
161 - 162 MR. AND MRS. J. ARDEN HARRIMAN
163 - 164 MR. AND MRS. JOSEPH HARRIMAN
165 - 166 MR. AND MRS. COOPER HEWITT
167 MR. McDOUGALL HAWKS
168 - 169 MR. AND MRS. CHARLES BETTS HILLHOUSE
170 MR. EUGENE HIGGINS

15

217	MR. GEORGE C. MUNZIG
218 - 219	MR. AND MRS. D. HENNEN MORRIS
220 - 221	MR. AND MRS. A. NEWBOLD MORRIS
222	MRS. WARD McALLISTER
223	MISS LOUISE WARD McALLISTER
224 - 225	MR. AND MRS. H. W. McVICKAR
226 - 227	MR. AND MRS. THOMAS NEWBOLD
228	MISS NEWBOLD
229	MR. WILLIAM HUDE NEILSON
230 - 231	MR. AND MRS. LANFEAR NORRIE
232 - 233	MR. AND MRS. GORDON NORRIE
234 - 235	MR. AND MRS. STEPHEN H. OLIN
236	MR. FRANCIS J. OTIS
237 - 238	MR. AND MRS. JAMES BROWN POTTER *née* HANDY
239 - 240	MR. AND MRS. FRANCIS KEY PENDLETON
241	MISS EVELYN PARSONS
242 - 243	THE MISSES GRETA AND MAMIE POMEROY
244 - 245	MR. AND MRS. HENRY PARISH, JR.
246	MR. FRANK L. POLK
247 - 248	MR. AND MRS. BENJAMIN C. PORTER
249 - 250	MR. AND MRS. CHARLES A. POST
251	MR. RICHARD PETERS
252 - 253	MR. AND MRS. EDWARD CLARKSON POTTER
254	MR. ARDEN MORRIS ROBBINS
255	MR. H. PELHAM ROBBINS
256 - 257	MR. AND MRS. P. LORILLARD RONALDS, JR.
258 - 259	MR. AND MRS. GEORGE L. RIVES
260	MR. REGINALD RONALDS
261 - 262	MR. AND MRS. CHARLES L. F. ROBINSON
263 - 264	MR. AND MRS. HENRY ASHER ROBBINS

17

316	MISS ANNA SANDS
317 - 318	MR. AND MRS. FREDERIC SHELDON
319 - 320	MR. AND MRS. FRANCIS B. STEVENS
321 - 322	MR. AND MRS. VICTOR SORCHAN
323 - 324	MR. AND MRS. JAMES A. STILLMAN
325 - 326	MR. AND MRS. HERBERT LIVINGSTON SATTERLEE
327 - 328	MR. AND MRS. J. FREDERIC TAMS
329 - 330	MR. AND MRS. EDWARD R. THOMAS
331 - 332	MR. AND MRS. WILLIAM R. TRAVERS
333 - 334	MR. AND MRS. JOHN S. TOOKER
335	MR. DIODATI THOMPSON
336 - 337	MR. AND MRS. ARCHIBALD GOURLIE THATCHER
338 - 339	MR. AND MRS. WILLIAM PAYNE THOMPSON
340 - 341	MR. AND MRS. BELMONT TIFFANY
342	MRS. PERRY TIFFANY
343 - 344	MR. AND MRS. J. LEE TAILER
345	MRS. VANDERBILT
346	MISS GLADYS VANDERBILT
347 - 348	MR. AND MRS. GEORGE W. VANDERBILT
349	MR. HAROLD STIRLING VANDERBILT
350 - 351	MR. AND MRS. FREDERICK W. VANDERBILT
352 - 353	MR. AND MRS. J. LAURENS VAN ALEN
354	MRS. ALEXANDER VAN RENSSELAER
355	MISS ALICE VAN RENSSELAER
356	MR. ROBERT B. VAN CORTLANDT
357 - 358	MR. AND MRS. W. FITZ HUGH WHITEHOUSE
359	MR. SHELDON WHITEHOUSE
360	MR. WILLIAM FITZ HUGH WHITEHOUSE, JR.
361 - 362	MR. AND MRS. J. NORMAN DE R. WHITEHOUSE

363 - 364	MR. AND MRS. J. J. WYSONG
365	MR. ALEXANDER S. WEBB, JR.
366 - 367	MR. AND MRS. EGERTON WEBB
368 - 369	MR. AND MRS. STANFORD WHITE
370	MR. CREIGHTON WEBB
371 - 372	MR. AND MRS. LUCIUS K. WILMERDING
373	MRS. BENJAMIN WELLES
374 - 375	MR. AND MRS. HAMILTON FISH WEBSTER
376 - 377	MR. AND MRS. FRANK S. WITHERBEE
378	MISS DOROTHY WHITNEY
379	MISS MARIE WINTHROP
380	MR. MATTHEW ASTOR WILKS
381 - 382	MR. AND MRS. GEORGE HENRY WARREN
383 - 384	MR. AND MRS. JOHN HOBART WARREN
385	MR. LLOYD WARREN
386	MR. HENRY ROGERS WINTHROP
387 - 388	MR. AND MRS. JAMES M. WATERBURY
389	MR. JAMES M. WATERBURY, JR.
390	MISS ELSIE WATERBURY
391 - 392	MR. AND MRS. LAWRENCE WATERBURY
393	MR. DELANO WEEKES
394 - 395	MR. AND MRS. ARTHUR WELLMAN
396	MR. BARTON WILLING
397	MR. FREDERIC BRONSON WINTHROP
398	MR. EGERTON L. WINTHROP
399 - 400	MR. AND MRS. EGERTON L. WINTHROP, JR.

List of the National Ultra=fashionable Set in the provincial cities and towns.

MRS. ASTOR

WASHINGTON, D. C.

MRS. VAN RENSSELAER CRUGER
MR. AND MRS. REGINALD DE KOVEN
MR. AND MRS. GEORGE PEABODY WETMORE
THE MISSES WETMORE
THE MESSRS. ROGERS AND WILLIAM WETMORE
MISS ALICE ROOSEVELT

CHICAGO, ILL.

MRS. POTTER PALMER
MR. AND MRS. HOBART CHATFIELD-TAYLOR
MR. JOSEPH LEITER

PITTSBURG, PA.

MR. HARRY KENDALL THAW

BOSTON, MASS.

MR. AND MRS. HOLLIS H. HUNNEWELL, JR.
MR. AND MRS. J. DE FOREST DANIELSON
MR. AND MRS. PRESCOTT LAWRENCE
MR. AND MRS. EUGENE VAN RENSSELAER THAYER
née BROOKS

HOLYOKE, MASS.
MR. RALPH RANLET

PHILADELPHIA, PA.
MR. AND MRS. E. MOORE ROBINSON
MR. AND MRS. WILLIAM E. CARTER
MR. AND MRS. CLARENCE W. DOLAN
MR. AND MRS. ANTHONY J. DREXEL
MR. AND MRS. JAMES FRANCIS SULLIVAN
MR. AND MRS. JOSEPH WIDENER
MR. AND MRS. GEORGE D. WIDENER
MR. EDWARD WILLING

DEVON, PA.
MR. WILLING SPENCER

BALTIMORE, MD.
THE CARROLLS OF CARROLLTON
MR. HENRY WALTERS
MR. WALTER DE CURZON POULTNEY
MR. WILLIAM LEHR
DR. AND MRS. HENRY BARTON JACOBS

VIRGINIA
MRS. LANGHORNE-SHAW

PROVIDENCE, R. I.
THE GODDARDS OF HOPETON HOUSE
MR. AND MRS. ROBERT IVES GAMMELL
MISS VIRGINIA GAMMELL
MR. AND MRS. WILLIAM G. ROELKER, JR. *née* COUDERT
MR. AND MRS. SHAW-SAFE *née* GAMMELL
MRS. JOHN NICHOLAS BROWN

GENESEO, N. Y.
THE WADSWORTH FAMILY

SAN FRANCISCO, CAL.
MR. AND MRS. PETER DONAHOE MARTIN
MR. LOUIS BRUGUIERE

BUFFALO, N. Y.
THE REV. AND MRS. GEORGE GRENVILLE MERRILL
née DRESSER

TEXAS
GENERAL AND MRS. FRED D. GRANT

THE PHILIPPINES
GENERAL AND MRS. HENRY C. CORBIN
LIEUTENANT DUNCAN ELLIOT

CHAPTER II.

Republican Coronets and the Golden Caste of Vere de Vere.

EWPORT, not the White House, is the supreme court of social appeals in the United States; Mrs. Astor, and not the wife of the President of the United States, is the first lady of the land, in the realm of fashion. Strange to narrate, in our free, democratic United States, almost within a decade, there has sprung up an exclusive social caste as valid at certain European courts as an hereditary titled aristocracy—a powerful class of ultra-fashionable multi-millionaires, who, at their present ratio of ascendency, bid fair to patronize royalty itself. Personages these are whom Edward VII. well might prefer to his own subjects for dinner companions and *intime* week-end house parties, to say nothing of their being the recipients of almost royal honors, not only at the palaces of sovereigns, but even aboard their own yachts, thus cheapening thrones in the eyes of subjects—these wearers of republican coronets and American strawberry leaves.

This all-powerful social trust, the ultra-fashionable set in American society, means, in reality, a combine of not more than four hundred families, aggregating about six hundred individuals, scattered through a very restricted number of cities of the Republic, only a few more, in fact, than the sum total of those cities which once claimed the honor of having been the birthplace of Homer. New York City, notably Newport-New York, Brooklyn, of course, being without representation, contributes a large quota of these coroneted families of the Republic; Washington half a dozen to a dozen in the winter season, not inclusive of the diplomats, who are *ex-officio* decreed by fashion *personæ gratæ* the world over; Boston and Baltimore, three or four, each, perhaps; Philadelphia eight, Providence six; Chicago three; Pittsburg one; Buffalo one; Virginia one; Devon, Pennsylvania, one; Texas one; Geneseo, N. Y., one; Holyoke, Mass., one; the Philippines two; South Carolina and Connecticut, both the land of proud colonial pedigrees, none; California, only one, unless Mr. Herman Oelrichs and Mr. and Mrs. Peter Donahoe Martin, *née* Oelrichs, can be accounted residents.

Philadelphia seems to be a decided vantage ground for a social aspirant to hail from, carefully taken statistics proving that within the two years past, more candidates from the Quaker City have been received into the smart set at Newport, than from any other city in the country, save the metropolis itself. The Philadelphian prides himself upon being what he terms well born; but birth and rank to the ultra-smart, alike in New York and London, are of the nature of accidents and do not belong to the essence of smartness. On the other hand, one may be enormously rich, yet preëminently dowdy; still there must be a nucleus of very rich people to form a substrate for a twentieth century smart set, whether in England or in the United States, and such a centralization of social forces in both these countries is to-day, to the fullest extent, a *fait accompli.*

Wealth, then, forms the principal ingredient entering into the composition of this big social trust whose subjective aim is pleasure, and whose objective one is to make a fine art of social life; but for enrollment in its membership, one's manners must also be *comme il faut,* and this is patent from the fact that some of the most opulent families on its lengthy waiting lists will not be deemed acceptable without undergoing a tedious apprenticeship, with more than a possibility of repeated and perhaps final failure. This doctrine of the relations and proportions of wealth as a factor in ultra-fashionable society is acquiesced in by Mr. Lispenard Stewart, a premier beau of society's smartest set. Another of society's *jeunesse dorée,* like Mr. Lispenard Stewart, a man of both wealth and patrician lineage, says, "When I go out to a social entertainment, I want to be amused; but it takes money to amuse me, and that is why I always enjoyed going to Mr. William C. Whitney's house, and why I look forward to Mr. James Henry Smith's entertainments under the same hospitable roof."

Mrs. Astor, on the other hand, with somewhat of a predilection for the old Knickerbocker and Colonial families, would state the case more conservatively than the majority of the men and women of her following. Aristocracy in America, we admit, consists in a measure of the possession of hereditary wealth; at all events, a family equipped with unabsorbed riches needs to get into its second generation on as short notice as possible. Note, for instance, the ascendant star in the social firmament of the William B. Leeds, the Edward R. Thomases, the Thomas Hastings, the William G. Roelkers, the Goadby Loews, and of the Spreckels, Bruguiere and M. H. De Young families of San Francisco.

Review the social triumphs of the past twelve months of the Clarence W. Dolans, the George and Joseph Wideners and the E. Moore Robinsons, also of Philadelphia. To go further back in the pages of the history of fashion, retrace the social evolution of the Pembroke Jones, only a few seasons ago occupying a cottage on Halidon Hill,

Newport, living very quietly and comparatively unknown to national society. The last two summers the Pembroke Jones were depended upon and looked up to as among the foremost entertainers of the Newport season, and the year before, they gave more fêtes and banquets on land and sea in honor of Consuelo, the Duchess of Marlborough, than any other members of the spectacular colony of the proud city by the sea.

To guarantee then the possession of good manners, a person does not need to produce a pedigree dating back to Mt. Ararat. The national smart set offers little scope for men encased in stiff Colonial and Knickerbocker types of manners with the aspirations of dukes and the fortunes of footmen.

Extraordinary personal beauty, such as that of Mrs. Charles Dana Gibson, Mrs. Benjamin C. Porter, Mrs. Langhorne-Shaw, Miss May Handy—Mr. and Mrs. Charles Dana Gibson being italicised as the handsomest married couple moving in New York society—and artistic genius, especially in the vocation of portrait painting, when backed by irreproachable manners, sometimes act as an *open sesame* into society's true inner circle. Let the distorted inference once for all be forestalled and corrected that the guest lists of Mrs. Astor's annual ball are made up of a solid phalanx of multi-millionaires. Among the portrait painters bidden to the last of these court functions were Mrs. Leslie

Cotton, Mr. Eliot Gregory, Mr. Harper Pennington, Mr. Muller-Ury, Mr. George C. Munzig and Mr. Charles Dana Gibson.

The 400 Coroneted families of the Republic— such a generalization or definition of the national social trust would not have been possible ten years ago, because it would have been split up into the disjointed social sets of various cities. Nowadays a person may be a social leader, in a provincial city like Boston, Chicago, Charleston, S. C., or San Francisco, and not necessarily have standing in *national* society, the ultra-fashionable set in the United States, whose claims must virtually be passed upon by Newport-New York and the Astor-Ogden Mills-Ogden Goelet-Cornelius Vanderbilt, Jr., social oligarchy, a court presentation more difficult to secure than one to a Buckingham Palace drawing-room or the Faubourg St. Germain. While any member of the ultra-smart Newport-New York set could find instant admission into the exclusive circles of the provincial cities, only a very small minority of the latter would readily receive invitations from *national* society, whose summer capitol is Newport.

Mrs. "Jack" Gardner and Mrs. J. Montgomery Sears, cultured and charming women, are the acknowledged leaders of Boston society, but it levies no diminution upon their social status in their own city, to explain that they do not belong to *national* society, the sublimated ultra-fashionable constituency of the United States, whereas, other Bostonians, for instance, Mr. and Mrs. E. Rollins Morse, Mr. and Mrs. J. De Forest Danielson, Mr. Hollis Hunnewell, Jr., Mr. Eugene Van Rensselaer Thayer and Mr. and Mrs. Prescott Lawrence, have complied with the conditions, and having been decreed eligible, are members of the national social trust.

For registration as one of the 400 Coroneted families of the Republic—that is, to be accounted ultra-smart, one is ordinarily supposed to have received an invitation to an Astor ball; and not to have dined at Mrs. Astor's virtually debars one from eminent leadership in that surpassing coterie known as national and international American society. It must always be borne in mind that it is the rank and number of one's dinner, and not of one's ball-room invitations, that the more vitally affect one's true ultra-smart status. Far from the truth would it be and an act of rank injustice even to intimate that the Astor family in any way caters to leadership or the swaying of social sceptres; at the same time, this exalted position is accorded them by both the tacit acclamation and etiquette of the combined social trust of the United States.

Smartness is fashion *incarné*, outwardly expressed by fitting artistic forms of dress, deportment and equipage. The following roll *d'honneur* of smartness, while representative, is not exhaustive, but is distinctively illustrative of those personages who, in their several vocations of society leaders, Wall Street magnates, authors, ecclesiastics, artists, or statesmen, would be recognized not only at home but abroad, as men and women of the highest cosmopolitan fashion, and equally valid in the drawing-rooms not only of New York and Newport, but of London, Paris, Rome, Vienna, St. Petersburg or Madrid. Among these striking examples of ultra-smartness may be cited Mrs. Astor, Mrs. Ogden Goelet, Mrs. Van Rensselaer Cruger, Mr. and Mrs. Cornelius Vanderbilt, Jr., Mr. and Mrs. William K. Vanderbilt, Mr. and Mrs. Benjamin C. Porter, Miss Natica Rives, Mr. and Mrs. Reginald Vanderbilt, Mr. Arthur Brisbane, Mr. and Mrs. William K. Vanderbilt, Jr., General and Mrs. Henry Lawrence Burnett, Creighton Webb, Mr. and Mrs. Reginald De Koven, Mr. and Mrs. George Jay Gould, Mr. Bourke Cochran, Mr. and Mrs. Philip M. Lydig, Mr. and Mrs. Charles Dana Gibson, the Marquise de Talleyrand-Périgord *née* Curtis, the Princess Ruspoli *née* Curtis, Mr. and Mrs. Levi P. Morton, Mr. and Mrs. Whitelaw Reid, Mr. Lispenard Stewart, Mrs. James P. Kernochan, Mr. and Mrs. Henry Clews, Miss Alice Van Rensselaer, Mr. James V. Parker, Mr. and Mrs. Reginald Rives, Mr. and Mrs. Ernest Iselin, Mrs. Van Rensselaer Johnson, Mr. and Mrs. Robert J. Collier, Mrs. Oscar F. Livingston, Mrs. Moses Taylor Campbell, Mrs. Burke-Roche, Miss Cynthia Burke-Roche, Mr. and Mrs. William A. M. Burden, Mrs. Richard Gambrill, Mrs. Lloyd Griscom, Mrs. Frederic Bronson, Mr. and Mrs. Herbert Livingston Satterlee, Mr. Walter de C. Poultney, Mr. and Mrs. Harry Payne Whitney, Mr. and Mrs. Thomas Hastings, Mr. and Mrs. Hobart Chatfield-Taylor, Mr. Eliot Gregory, Mr. and Mrs. John R. Drexel, Mr. T. Suffern Tailer, Miss Rosamond Street, Mr. and Mrs. Royal Phelps Carroll, Miss Anna Tooker Best, Mr. and Mrs. Edmund L. Baylies, Mr. and Mrs. Charles Carroll, Mr. and Mrs. Henry A. C. Taylor, Miss Evelyn Parsons, Mr. and Mrs. Oliver H. P. Belmont, Jay Coogan, Mr. Charles de L. Oelrichs, Mr. and Mrs. Sidney J. Smith, Miss d'Acosta, Col. and Mrs. John Jacob Astor, Miss Alice Babcock, Miss Marion Haven, Mr. and Mrs. Leslie Cotton, Mr. and Mrs. Chauncey M. Depew, Miss Laura Patterson Swan, Mr. and Mrs. Elisha Dyer, Jr., and Mr. Harold Stirling Vanderbilt.

Let it be once for all premised that the shibboleths, "the 150," "the 400" and "the 600" are never used by the members of the ultra-smart set themselves, and that in social life, to talk of the 150 or the 400 argues one's self utterly outside the pale of these designations. The slogans, the 150 and the 400, are used in this work merely as approximations; for instance, the number of fashionable folk who are always *en evidence* and the most ambitious to carry on the really hard work incurred by the treadmill of society number 150 more closely than any other figures. The mystical number, 150, thus symbolizes the true innermost circle of fashion. As Mrs. John R. Drexel, one of the social leaders in New York and Newport's smartest set, said the other day, "This having to keep *en evidence* the year round, we society women simply drop down in harness."

To be seen at an occasional Astor ball, or even at an Astor dinner, and at no other dinners of importance the rest of the year, will not enroll one among the 150. Time was when a family, fortified by a proud Knickerbocker panoply and backed by a fortune in keeping, could sit apart like the gods upon Olympus, taking little active part in society; but, on the contrary, being ministered to by it, and emerge occasionally from a glorious obscurity by giving a crush reception, with a blockade of carriages of the ultra-fashionable; but the old order passeth away. If a family is not willing to do the work of society in regular American fashion every month and every day in the year, it is relegated to the background. I am glad to see that some of the heirs of the late William C. Schermerhorn are beginning to ponder on these themes.

In European society, which is based upon an hereditary aristocracy, the whole family is accounted fashionable, although one of its daughters, ignoring society altogether, may give the bent of her energies to charities, another to music, and a third to writing, like Lady Sarah Wilson, for instance, who went down into the Transvaal as a newspaper war correspondent. In the United States, on the contrary, the rebound from conservatism is so accentuated that a solitary individual may be the only member of a family decreed fashionable. Social talent, it must be borne in mind, is rightly accounted as much of an inborn gift as a talent for portrait painting or sculpture. The viceregal leaders under Mrs. Astor of the 150, which is the smartest set in the United States, are Mrs. Ogden Mills, Mrs. John Jacob Astor, Mrs. Cornelius Vanderbilt, Jr., and Mrs. Ogden Goelet. Mrs. Ogden Mills can really plume herself on having the most exclusive house in America. For her balls, there is no scurrying around to hunt up dancing young men and women, who are never seen at an ultra-smart dinner, to fill out; she has no assistant "manager" for her ball-room guest list, and begging around in behalf of friends is practically useless.

The "400" in this the American Peerage, is composed of very fashionable people, a number of whom have received the fully accredited Astor and Ogden Mills social *cachet*. There are two grades of social acceptance represented by the 400, as will be readily seen by anyone understanding the structure of society. To designate to what persons the second grade applies would be invidious, besides a whole group of these individuals are making rapid social headway, and who knows but they may arrive any day within the charmed circle of the 150.

The greatest genius America has produced for planning balls and dinners and *al fresco* routs, as well as for ranging fashionable society into a judiciously blended exclusive caste was the late Mr. Ward McAllister. Mr. McAllister had planned for me the details of an unique charity fête, besides outlining the order for the decorations, musical programme and *tout ensemble* of a golden wedding for some near relatives of mine, at which I was to be master of ceremonies. And so, when the combined newspaper and magazine press of the country was firing its fusilades at Mr. McAllister's book—*Society, as I Have Found It*—I presented him with a monograph, written by myself, bringing out into bold relief what few strong points were latent in the book. Mr. McAllister's enthusiasm was so great that he went personally to the editor of the New York *Herald* and had my eulogies of his book inserted in its columns in an article covering nearly a page. The announcement was placarded in huge lettering on the bill-boards of all the elevated railroad stations in town—"Read next Sunday's *Herald*. The Rev. Dr. C. W. de Lyon

Nichols, Ward McAllister's first Apostle on the Philosophy of Society, and Mrs. James Brown Potter on Women in India."

But the register of ultra-smart people has changed a good deal since Mr. McAllister's day, although Mrs. Astor still remains the leader, with a national attitude of importance now superadded to such regency. And wealth and the highest fashion have become so much more centralized in Newport every year, that it has become as imperative for a social aspirant's claims to be passed upon by Newport, as it was for a potentate of the era of Charlemagne to go to St. Peter's, Rome, for coronation!

CHAPTER III.

HE ultra-smart man is ordinarily rated as expending from one to three thousand dollars a year for clothes, albeit the tailor bills of Col. John Jacob Astor, who is always dressed every inch the gentleman, would, beyond gainsay, fall below the thousand dollar low-water mark. As noticeably well dressed men, this monograph brevets Mr. Elisha Dyer, Jr., sometimes pointed out as "the best-dressed man at Newport;" Henry C. Clews, Jr., Henry Symes Lehr, Woodbury Kane, James Henry Smith, T. Suffern Tailer, Hon. Levi P. Morton, Reginald Ronalds, Herbert Livingston Satterlee, James V. Parker, Whitney Warren, H. McK. Twombly, Stanford White, W. Fitz Hugh Whitehouse, George J. Gould, R. T. Wilson, Jr., M. Orme Wilson, Harry Havemeyer, James A. Stillman, Alphonse de Navarro, Royal Phelps Carroll, R. H. I. Goddard, Adrian Iselin, Jr., Stanley Mortimer, Charles A. Munn, Robert Ives Gammell, James R. Keene, Charles H. Marshall, Oliver Harriman, Jr., Robert J. Collier, A. Newbold Morris, W. Watts Sherman,

Prescott Lawrence, Lispenard Stewart, William B. Cutting, August Belmont, Senator William A. Clark, Henry Siegel, William P. Thompson, Rutherford Stuyvesant, Robert Livingston Gerry, William K. Vanderbilt, Robert Walton Goelet, Henry Parish, Jr., Dr. Seward Webb, Edward R. Thomas, Townsend Burden, Pembroke Jones, Richard Peters, Egerton L. Winthrop, Sr., Egerton L. Winthrop, Jr., Rhinelander Stewart, Robert B. Van Cortlandt, Oliver H. P. Belmont, Arthur Brisbane, J. Abercrombie Burden, Sr., J. Abercrombie Burden, Jr., William A. Duer, T. J. Oakley Rhinelander, David Wolfe Bishop, W. Starr Miller, Geo. B. De Forest, Charles Dana Gibson, F. O. Beach, William Douglas Sloane, Alfred G. Vanderbilt, Jay Coogan and Reginald Vanderbilt.

To Mr. Henry C. Clews, Jr., is accorded the royal accolade of being the foremost among ultra-smart amateurs in creating fashions in dress for men. To Mr. Clews is referred the invention of the folded cuff, to say nothing of a whole consignment of fancy waistcoats. Furthermore, Mr. Clews was the first to introduce at Newport, from Paris, the Charvet, or, as it is now Americanized, "Imandt Grand Prix" vest. On this occasion, the international tennis tournament at Newport, Mr. Clews wore a suit of purplish gray cheviot, with a double-breasted vest of bright brocaded purple satin, a long flowing scarf, of a bit brighter shade of purple, a white felt *chapeau-la-ville* hat, with heavy folds of purple corded-silk girded around it. His boutonnière consisted of a light purple, exotic shade of what is called "snowball," in a New England old wives' garden. A Grand Prix vest is always cut double-breasted and made without any buttons visible. Its material, usually purple corded silk, or silk poplin of the same hue, comports well with a frock coat, of course, and even with a fancy light-colored sack coat on gala occasions,

While among ultra-fashionable women, reactions ever and anon set in for a while against the flamboyant and conspicuous in dress, with the men, on the contrary, a steadily increasing picturesqueness and poetic license in personal attire are *en règle*. This emancipation of the male sex from the sombre effects and dead-level monochrome of attire which held sway only a few years ago is largely due to the advent of the Summer man among us. Of the Summer fine art of dressing Mr. Clarence H. Mackay ranks as an exponent. For dining at home at one's country seat in summer, nothing is cooler, more novel or half so *chic* as a light Tuxedo suit of white silk basket-weave, plain twilled silk, or white duck; Mr. Mackay has fully a dozen of such outfits.

For summer riding and shooting habits, Mr. Woodbury Kane's, Foxhall Keene's and Craig Wadsworth's style is usually of the latest. The

Rev. Dr. Rainsford's golf and tennis suits of a few seasons ago have passed into sartorial history of a *sui generis* content. Certainly, a golf suit was never before or since pressed into service for so great a variety of social functions by a single individual. Anent of shooting coats—the really modish ones are cut with a gap in the back—a new common-sense wrinkle, to insure perfect freedom in handling a gun. The use of the pink hunting-coat, which I have seen worn, alike on the Roman Campagna and in Windsor Forest, is really as general among the polite nations of the Occident as the adoption of French as the court language of the world. A man invited to a fashionable hunt, such as one of P. F. Collier's at Newport, for instance, if punctilious about how he is groomed, should procure a single-breasted frock hunting-coat, cut long, with full skirts and made of Oxford gray or dark-brown mixed goods.

Men's predilections for special features in personal attire naturally vary. Mr. Elbridge T. Gerry's fancies entwine themselves around a sealskin cap; Mr. Townsend Burden and Mr. Henry Siegel, both particularly well-groomed men, have a penchant for foot-gear, often having stowed away in their wardrobes as many as forty pairs of new shoes of superior quality and workmanship. The caprice of Mrs. Burden's kinsman, Mr. Walter de Curzon Poultney, Baltimore's aristocratic and veteran beau of society runs to turquoise rings and *costume de bain*, his record in the cut and translucency of bathing habiliments at our American Trouville a season or two ago having inscribed Mr. Poultney's name upon the pages of deathless fame of the nation's Sartor Resartus.

But to take up an approximate inventory of an ultra-smart man's wardrobe : It contains a fur-lined top coat for the opera; an Inverness fur-lined, without the fur showing; a Chesterfield, in black or dark gray, or a Newmarket, to be worn over dress clothes ordinarily; a long, loose sack over-coat, silk-faced for Spring and early Autumn; a double-breasted Newmarket, a single-breasted Prince Henry coat, a Strand coat, which is single-breasted with tails; rain and steamer coats, yachting suits, a double-breasted ulster, made of home-spun; golf costumes and a short covert coat for between seasons. For golfing, only a few incurable Anglomaniacs among our society men still persist in wearing Knickerbockers with rough stockings and Norfolk jackets, the outfit being voted exasperatingly trying in midsummer. Driving and automobile coats, of course, vary with the season. For four-in-hand driving, the Newmarket coat must disport a flaring skirt.

In top coats *de luxe*, nothing in New York City has been worn comparable with Senator William A. Clark's sable-lined one, for which he drew his cheque for upward of two thousand dollars. Furthermore, it was not an imported garment. In general, it is a fallacy, jointly flattering to the invention of one or two of the society reporters on the daily papers, and the tissue of lies told by certain society folk themselves departing for Europe, misleading the general public into believing that more than six out of a dozen of our men of fashion go over to London for clothes. Mr. Craig Wadsworth, William B. Cutting, F. O. Beach, Richard Peters, Harry and Fred Havemeyer, have been for years patrons of Poole and Hill Bros., of London, but William K. Vanderbilt, Cornelius Vanderbilt, Col. John Jacob Astor, Townsend Burden, and scores of other men of equal standing in our great world, favor, to a large extent, with their patronage the tailoring shops of Fifth Avenue and a culled out few of its intersecting thoroughfares in the Thirtieth streets.

The sturdy independence of excessive English domination in male attire was seldom as pointedly exhibited as by the rejection, not long ago, of the single-breasted frock coat which King Edward, then Prince of Wales, tried to create, and which was afterward exposed in the United States to be, in reality, the conventional dress coat of a Church of England bishop; at all events, our leaders of the mode tabooed it as essentially unbecoming, giving as it did to a man an ecclesiastical and professional aspect, when wishing, above all, to look like a Wall Street magnate. At the other horn of a somewhat similar sartorial dilemma, people untutored in the clothes philosophy, fall into the ludicrous blunder of thinking that because the color of a Grand Prix waistcoat is purple it must be regarded as a vestment of the Church. Apropos of purple, which Elisha Dyer and Harry Lehr ever and anon affect in their neckwear, the only purple straw hat ever worn at our national summer capitol, was that of a European ecclesiastic, who was told in defence of his chapeau, which riveted attention, that "nothing was ever conspicuous at Newport."

A man or woman brought into social contact with the "magic circle" needs to be solidly well placed socially, to indulge in inventive vagaries in dress, or make the slightest semblance of setting a fashion. The *bon mot* I once heard uttered at the Waldorf-Astoria, that a New Yorker could, at a glance, detect a man from the provinces by his hat, contained more than a half-truth. To such aspirants outside of the Brahmin caste, it needs to be iterated and reiterated that the majority of men, fitted to be censors of taste, are wearing fobs more than watch chains and quiet seal rings made entirely of dead gold, without stones set in them. A conspicuous watch chain, although a concentrated effort is being made in some of the European capitols to bring them into vogue again, placards a man as vulgar, and the stouter his girth the more vulgar, for no one in his senses is eager to label an *embonpoint*. The late Mr. Ward McAllister was not a well-dressed man, but he was particularly strenuous in his monitions on this latter point.

Apropos of *bijouterie*, by no means every man of fashion invests in costly pearls for scarf-pins or sleeve-buttons; in common with some of the women of the smart-set, they wear the best artificial pearls New York or Paris affords—the Frederic fishskin pearls.

Unlike, perhaps, a Rockefeller on his way to teach a Bible class of a Sunday morning, the man of highest fashion is not seen so often as he was a year or two ago, wearing his frock coat and silk hat to church on Sunday morning; he is quite as likely to appear in English walking coat and even a Derby hat. The idea of dressing up in one's best of a Sunday morning, like a *ci-devant* Easter parade, is now relegated to the class of men who buy their clothes in Eighth avenue, and to men of aldermanic proportions, who disport themselves in suits of big plaid patterns on week days. We will condone Mr. Thomas Suffern Tailer's green suits of clothes at Newport last season, for they had very modish transatlantic precedents to fall back upon, besides, when one has the blood of both a Suffern and a Tailer coursing through his veins, he can do a variety of things with impunity. That far-descended beau of society, Mr. James V. Parker, has even been charged with the introduction of that nondescript known as the polka-dot collar.

One of the freshest novelties, both in London and at Newport, the past season was the English straw hat. Only two or three of them were seen at Newport, but one or two of those were worn by Vanderbilts. These hats are of gray and white mixed straw, with the brim lined with black straw, which relieves the glaring white effect which an Englishman dislikes in a straw hat, and the whole chapeau has the virtue of not soiling easily amid the soot of London or the soft coal atmosphere of New York City. The hat is the one known as the Lansdowne.

Mr. Elisha Dyer, Jr., is sometimes pointed out as the best dressed man at Newport. Whether the encomium be fully accredited or not, both Mr. Dyer and Mr. Lispenard Stewart are always so well dressed, wearing nothing too voyant or conspicuous, and the general effect harmonizes so well that one is at a loss to fathom what makes them so well dressed. Simplicity and repose, however, were the norm of the Greek ideal of beauty.

CHAPTER IV.

Dress and American Beauties.

RS. JOHN R. DREXEL, who came back from Europe last summer, having been the recipient of almost royal honors from Edward VII. and his court, and whose steamer luggage consisted mostly of boxes piled high with the freshest creations of Paquin, Doucet and other *couturières* and modistes of the Rue de la Paix, was adjudged not only one of the best gowned, but also one of the most beautiful women at Newport, in both these respects carrying off equal encomiums with Mrs. Philip Lydig and Mrs. Moore Robinson.

Mrs. Drexel, who is the smartest of any of the women of the Drexel families, has always been remarked for her thrift and good practical common sense, and has even been known to have a gown made over, if she has taken a decided fancy to it. It was she who uttered the somewhat famous pronunciamento on dress, "We must attain simplicity; we can no longer go about dressed like the demimonde." Mrs. Drexel's and Mrs. Lydig's portraits appear in the *recherché* American Beauty Book, arranged by Miss Isabella Cameron, a daughter of the late Sir Roderick Cameron.

Other women of national repute in the world of fashion, who may be cited as combining good dressing with personal beauty to a noticeable degree, are Mrs. John Jacob Astor, Mrs. Clarence H. Mackay, Mrs. Lorillard Spencer, Mrs. Burke-Roche, Miss Cynthia Burke-Roche, Mrs. Cornelius Vanderbilt, Jr., Mrs. James Brown Potter *née* Handy, Mrs. Benjamin C. Porter, Mrs. Herman Oelrichs, Mrs. Van Rensselaer Cruger, Mrs. Peter D. Martin *née* Oelrichs, Mrs. E. Moore Robinson, Mrs. Oscar Livingston, Mrs. James Francis Sullivan, of Philadelphia; Mrs. Henry Clews, Miss Natica Rives, Miss Alice Blight, Mrs. Edward R. Thomas, Mrs. Benjamin Thaw, Mrs. William B. Leeds, Mrs. Henry L. Burnett, Miss Natalie Storrs Wells, Mrs. Henry Siegel, Mrs. William K. Vanderbilt, Jr., Miss Gwendolin Burden, Mrs. Oliver Harriman, Miss Anna Tooker Best, Mrs. George Jay Gould, Mrs. Leslie Cotton, Miss Eleanor Jay, Mrs. J. Lee Tailer, Miss Violet Cruger, Mrs. Charles Dana Gibson, Mrs. Langhorne-Shaw, Mrs. Robert Goelet *née* Whelen, Miss Rosamond Street, Mrs. Norman Whitehouse, Miss Mathilde Townsend, Mrs. John A. de Zérèga, Mrs. Payne Whitney, Miss Isabella Cameron, Mrs. Clark Culver, Mrs. William Payne Thompson, Mrs. De Lancey Kountze, Mrs. Cass Canfield, Mrs. Reginald Brooks, Mrs. Jacob Berry, Miss Gladys Berry,

Miss Alice Babcock, Mrs. William G. Roelker, Jr.
née Coudert; Mrs. Edwin Gould, Mrs. Cortland
Field Bishop *née* Bend, Miss Maud Livingston,
Mrs. Adolph Ladenburg, Mrs. Edgar Barclay Car-
roll, Mrs. Charles H. Marshall, Mrs. Reginald Van-
derbilt, Mrs. Fred D. Grant, Mrs. James Cogswell
Converse *née* Berry, Mrs. Oakley Rhinelander,
Mrs. Potter Palmer, Mrs. Sidney J. Smith, the
Misses Ogden Mills and Mrs. W. Watts Sherman.

Mrs. John Jacob Astor, Mrs. Charles Dana
Gibson, Mrs. Benjamin C. Porter, Mrs. Lee Tailer,
Mrs. Lorillard Spencer, Mrs. Burke-Roche, Mrs.
Van Rensselaer Cruger, Mrs. Clarence Mackay and
Mrs. James Brown Potter *née* Handy, are singled
out by artists as "the classical and aristocratic
beauties."

Let royal coffers be what they may, the col-
lective contents of the jewel caskets of the ultra-
fashionable set in New York society approximate
closely to one hundred and seventy millions of dollars. Upwards of half a dozen women, notably
Mrs. Astor, Mrs. Vanderbilt, Mrs. Oliver H. P.
Belmont, and Mrs. William K. Vanderbilt, Jr.,
each have a million dollars invested in these arti-
cles for personal adornment. Among women
whose *bijouterie* foot up in value closely to eight
hundred thousand dollars, may be cited Mrs. Ogden
Goelet, Mrs. Orme Wilson, and Mrs. Herman
Oelrichs.

47

Others worthy of being entered as prize exhibitors at any lapidary's vanity fair, are Mrs. Levi P. Morton, Mrs. George Jay Gould, Mrs. Henry Siegel, Mrs. Alfred G. Vanderbilt, Mrs. J. Abercrombie Burden, Sr., Mrs. John R. Drexel, Mrs. W. Starr Miller, Mrs. George W. Vanderbilt, Mrs. William Douglas Sloane, Mrs. Harry Payne Whitney, Mrs. Payne Whitney, Mrs. Edwin Gould, Mrs. Stuyvesant Fish and Mrs. Cornelius Vanderbilt, Jr.

But the ultra-smart and old Father Neptune have a combine working against them, for the Frederic fish-skin pearl, the cleverest imitation under the sun, is having a great vogue. These artificial pearls, more beautiful than some of the real ones, are sometimes worn by fashionable women along with their others, when aiming at especially grand effects in dressing, or when not wishing to bother with the risk of carrying their genuine pearls along with them when traveling.

Mrs. Ogden Goelet's famous dog collar with its solitaire black pearl in the centre, probably eclipses any other article of personal adornment in real pearls in this country since Mrs. Oliver Belmont's wedding present of her ropes of pearls to her daughter, the Duchess of Marlborough; and both have been estimated as highly as two hundred thousand dollars in value. Mrs. Van Rensselaer Cruger was one of the first women of the smart set to appear with long ropes of Oriental pearls, in the horseshoe tier of the Metropolitan Opera boxes, and she wears them in both of her exquisite portraits by Sargent and Benjamin C. Porter. Mrs. Oscar Livingston is often envied her old family heirlooms in black pearls.

While ropes of Oriental pearls of almost priceless purity enchain the necks and shoulders of the smartest set, the coronets of diamonds worn at the opera cost on the average not more than twenty thousand dollars. Of a few of the more imposing tiaras, however, each of the pear-shaped brilliants capping the apex could easily command five thousand dollars. If a woman aspires to regal effects in evening dress, besides her diamond tiara, a corsage piece of diamonds, valued at, say, seventy-five thousand dollars, is requisite. Mrs. John R. Drexel's glittering sheen of sunbursts, disposed in this fashion, has passed into social history, illustrating as it does a fundamental canon of high art, whether in church decoration or that of one's house or person, that artistic ornaments should represent, as often as possible, objects in nature.

The rich necklace of Holbein work presented by the English ambassador to the Empress Josephine at the time of her marriage to Napoleon I., now graces the jewel casket of Mrs. Henry Siegel, one of the most beautiful and accomplished women of New York society, whose house in Park Lane during the recent London season was much frequented by peers and peeresses of the realm. A brooch, once belonging to Mary, Duchess of Cambridge, the mother of the late Duke, has also come into Mrs. Siegel's possession. It is of old mine diamonds, in the old crown setting of a hundred and fifty years ago. Mrs. Siegel also has souvenirs of Marie Antoinette in her jewel casket.

To Mrs. Burke-Roche, the smartest horsewoman in the United States, one must look for the technically correct thing in riding habits. Those worn by her at Newport, customarily made of linen, are in tan, white and gray shades, Mrs. John Jacob Astor, Mrs. Ogden Mills, Mrs. Herman Oelrichs, Mrs. George Jay Gould, Mrs. Stuyvesant Fish, Mrs. Clarence Mackay, Mrs. Henry S. Lehr, and Mrs. William Watts Sherman are superbly gowned women. Mrs. John Jacob Astor, in keeping with the precedent set by her mother-in-law, Mrs. Astor, owes some of her felicitous creations in the line of toilettes to Parisian *couturières*, of whom at the present are Paquin, Callot, and the Maison Beer. The fur cloaks of Mrs. John Jacob Astor and of Mrs. Stuyvesant Fish, another frequent patroness of Parisian dressmakers, are of almost fabulous costliness and elegance. Mrs. Sidney Smith, on the other hand, evinces artistic cleverness of a high order in designing some of her own most admired gowns, several of them having been mistaken for Parisian creations.

A number of conspicuously smart women, I regret to aver, are overbearing and difficult in the extreme to have dealings with in gowns and hats. A woman who will draw her cheque perhaps for thousands of dollars, for the services of a soloist from the Metropolitan Opera for a musicale, as likely as not, will dicker with her dressmaker to an exasperating degree about the cost of making a gown.

"You must stop to consider the value of our name to you," she will argue when haggling about the price of a gown. "A New York firm will dress me for nothing," a Newport cottager plead, a short time ago, with a Summer dressmaker. In fact, a woman, who is making a fortune as a dressmaker, said to me, "Deliver me from the smart set; give me a new rich woman from the upper West side every time for a customer."

Of Chicago ultra-fashionables, no two are more handsomely gowned than Mrs. Potter Palmer and Mrs. Arthur Caton, Mrs. Palmer's bills for clothes having been rated as high as ten thousand a year. Of Philadelphians, the women who lead the van in the fine art of dressing are Mrs. Moore Robinson, Mrs. William E. Carter, Mrs. James Francis Sullivan and Mrs. Joseph Widener.

The three reigning dowagers of highest fashion in America are Mrs. Astor, Mrs. James P. Kernochan and Mrs. R. T. Wilson, Sr.; but unlike the ultra-smart London dowager, not any one of this trio of American grand dames is ever guilty of committing anachronisms in dress. In fact, Newport-New York women are the best dressed women in the world. Dress not only heightens virtue, but actually creates beauty nowadays. This high æsthetic doctrine was seldom so vividly exemplified as by the fancy dress costumes worn at Mrs. Herman Oelrich's white ball, the crowning event of this Newport season, and in which Mrs. Osborn reached her apotheosis as a dressmaker to the smart set.

Reverting again to beauty, which is always akin to dress, one reason why New York society has been obliged to ransack Philadelphia, Baltimore, the whole solid South and the Pacific Slope for beautiful women is because such a strong infusion of coarse Holland Dutch market gardening blood coursed through the veins of established metropolitan society up to a decade ago.

A notable and happy international marital alliance was that of Sir George and Lady Frankland *née* di Zérèga. The late Lady Frankland, in whose honor a large and highly artistic memorial window was placed by her family in the Episcopal church at Westchester, N. Y., was the only daughter of Mr. and Mrs. John A. di Zérèga. Mrs. di Zérèga, a woman of rare and varied accomplishments, is exceedingly pretty and always well gowned, the

52

same encomiums also being merited by her nieces, Mrs. Stewart Pullman West *née* di Zérèga, Mrs. James Cogswell Converse *née* Berry and Miss Gladys Berry. No other woman in New York society possesses more of that distinctive type of elegance which stamps the Faubourg Saint Germain than Mrs. John A. di Zérèga. She is a sister of Mr. Jacob Berry, the well-known banker, who married one of the Monumental City's belles. The di Zérèga family is also connected by marriage with the titled Pelham-Clintons of England. The little coterie, of which Mrs. di Zérèga and her family connections form the leaders, is exclusive, in the best sense of the term, an education to one who wishes to acquire manners, and bears the hall-marks of a genuine *salon* quality.

Two young society débutantes of blue-blooded Maryland antecedents and related to several of Baltimore's social leaders—the Misses McLean, the daughters of Mr. and Mrs. Donald McLean, of this city, are everywhere remarked for their beauty, natural style and tasteful dressing. Apropos of Baltimore, Mrs. Lee Tailer, Mrs. William E. Carter *née* Polk, and Mrs. Francis B. Stevens, were Monumental City belles and are adepts in the fine art of personal attire. Baltimore women, from time immemorial, I am happy to record, have paid more attention to the cosmetics than to the Cosmos.

Newport's spectacular quintette of young society belles is just now composed of Miss Natica Rives, who has such an extraordinary *penchant* for picture hats, and is patrician to her finger tips; Miss Cynthia Burke-Roche, who should follow the sartorial example of her beautiful mother and not essay little mannerisms in dress; Miss Gwendolin Burden, the younger daughter of the fearfully and wonderfully well-dressed Townsend Burden family; the beautiful Miss Edith Colford, whose relationship to a former social leader who once lived in a marble palace in Fifth avenue, society chroniclers seem to have overlooked, and Miss Anna Tooker Best, niece of Mr. Gabriel Mead Tooker, of Newport and Paris, and own cousin to Mrs. Whitney Warren, whose first formal appearance in society was made at one of Mrs. Astor's balls.

The Misses Ogden Mills, always gowned in keeping with the most approved Parisian and London refinements of the art, would be taken anywhere for English young women. Both comely and *distingué*, in their patrician expression of visage and in their bearing, they reflect the Royal House of Bruce lineage of their father, Mr. Ogden Mills coupled with the aureole of their maternal Livingston ancestry.

CHAPTER V.

RE you shoddy, or old family ? Shoddy pays the best." An over-candid servant, looking for a place the other day, put the question to the chatelaine of a Fifth Avenue mansion. Wealth is such a potent factor in ultra-fashionable life that the Phillistine is very apt to topple over to the extreme and make bold to say that it is all a matter of crass, crude riches and that scarcely any patrician lineages can be deciphered among the ultra-smart, and furthermore, that plutocrats do not care a picayune for that sort of stilted bagatelle.

In refutation of this, the Royal College of Arms of London is more than half supported by wealthy Americans, emulous of having their pedigrees trailed back to Domesday Book, or at least to kings and princes of the royal blood. Families who will not bother to join the Colonial Dames or that sort of thing, will *sub rosa* expend hundreds and thousands of dollars in having their European as well as American antecedents exploited for their own private self-content. Mr. J. Pierpont Morgan,

Mr. E. D. Morgan and Mrs. Herbert Livingston Satterlee are scions of a dynasty of Welsh kings, the founder of which was Gynned Cymric, king of all Wales 605, A. D. Mr. Morgan can by right use eighteen quarterings on his shield, but by choice shows only twelve. Daniel N. Morgan, ex-Treasurer of the United States, belongs to the same clan.

Furthermore, we are able to muster with ease a roll *d'honneur* of ultra-fashionable folk whose lineages will bear close inspection under the X-rays of the genealogical searchlight, notably those of Mr. and Mrs. Lorillard Spencer, Mr. and Mrs. Elbridge T. Gerry *née* Livingston, Mrs. George W. Vanderbilt *née* Dresser, Mrs. Van Rensselaer Cruger, Mr. and Mrs. Royal Phelps Carroll, Mr. and Mrs. Charles Carroll, Mrs. Ogden Mills, James V. Parker, Mrs. Townsend Burden, Mrs. Henry Symes Lehr, Mrs. James P. Kernochan, Mrs. Oscar Livingston, Mrs. James Francis Sullivan, Mr. and Mrs. T. J. Oakley Rhinelander, Stuyvesant Le Roy, Colonel William Jay, Mr. and Mrs. W. Bayard Cutting, Mr. and Mrs. R. Fulton Cutting, Thomas Suffern Tailer, General and Mrs. Henry Lawrence Burnett, Mr. and Mrs. Oliver H. P. Belmont, Mr. and Mrs. W. Watts Sherman, Mr. and Mrs. Sidney J. Smith *née* Tailer, Mrs. Robert Goelet *née* Warren, Whitney Warren, Mrs. Henry Siegel *née* Vaughan, Francis Burton Harrison, Walter de Curzon Poultney, Mrs. Henry Parish, Jr. *née* Ludlow, Frederic

Diodati Thompson, Mr. and Mrs. Stuyvesant Fish, Mrs. Ward McAllister, Miss Ward McAllister, Mrs. Astor, Col. and Mrs. John Jacob Astor, Mr. and Mrs. Spencer Trask, William Jay Schieffelin, Mr. and Mrs. Edmund L. Baylies, Rawlins Cottenet, W. Fitz Hugh Whitehouse, Worthington Whitehouse, Mrs. Richard McCreery *née* Kip, James J. Van Alen, Lispenard Stewart, Mrs. Frank S. Witherbee, Mr. and Mrs. Prescott Lawrence *née* Bulkley, Edward H. Bulkley, Louis F. Holbrook Betts, Barton Willing, Mrs. Clarence H. Mackay, Mrs. James Abercrombie Burden, Mrs. James Brown Potter *née* Handy, Mrs. Moses Taylor Campbell *née* De Ruyter, Miss Cynthia Burke-Roche, Winthrop Rutherfurd, Mrs. and Mrs. Frederic Sheldon, J. Roosevelt Roosevelt, Charles Astor Bristed, Mr. and Mrs. Hamilton Fish Webster, Mrs. Frederic Bronson, George Jay Gould, Egerton L. Winthrop, Frederic Bronson Winthrop, Robert B. Van Cortlandt, William K. Vanderbilt, Jr., George Livingston Nichols, Mr. and Mrs. Charles Frederick Hoffman *née* Preston, Eugene Van Rensselaer Thayer, Miss Alice Van Rensselaer, Mrs. Adolph Ladenburg, *née* Stevens, Miss Alice Roosevelt, Mrs. Langhorne-Shaw, Miss Laura Patterson Swan, Acosta Nichols, Miss Natica Rives, Mrs. Louis L. Lorillard *née* Beeckman, R. Livingston Beeckman, Francis Key Pendleton, Mrs. Vanderbilt and the Marquise de Talleyrand-Périgord *née* Curtis.

Mrs. Astor, who was a Schermerhorn, besides having a good old English and Colonial Barclay ancestral backing, traces her lineage to King James I. of Scotland. Colonel John Jacob Astor's pedigree is emblazoned by the escutcheons of two Kings James I. of Scotland and Hugh Capet of France, from the latter of whom, supplemented by generation upon generation of gentility, Mrs. John Jacob Astor, one of the most far-descended as well as beautiful leaders of the ultra-smart set in the United States, derives her patrician cast of family type. Ogden Mills, Mrs. Vanderbilt, Mrs. Oscar Livingston, Mrs. James Francis Sullivan, of Philadelphia, Mrs. Frank S. Witherbee, Lispenard Stewart, James Laurens Van Alen, Mrs. Royal Phelps Carroll and Mrs. Vanderbilt descend gracefully from kings.

The name of Admiral De Ruyter graces the topmost bough of the family tree of Mrs. Moses Taylor Campbell, *née* De Ruyter, one of the smart young matrons of Mrs. Stuyvesant Fish's immediate coterie. Mrs. Campbell's mother was a Miss Cromwell, daughter of the late Charles Cromwell, Esq., of New York, and Manursing Island, Rye, a descendant of Oliver Cromwell. Oddly enough, Admiral De Ruyter and Oliver Cromwell fought one another in the North Sea. Mrs. Charles Cromwell, Mrs. Campbell's mother, was a Miss Brooks, in direct line from Governor Bradford; and the

Brooks mansion is to this day the aristocratic old chateau of Bridgeport, Connecticut. The family of Mr. H. Mortimer Brooks, several generations back, was allied to this proud race of Brookses.

Mrs. Oliver H. P. Belmont, Mrs. Clarence H. Mackay, Mrs. Frederic Bronson, William K. Vanderbilt, Jr., and Harold Stirling Vanderbilt can justly plume themselves on being scions of Lord Stirling. Mrs. Belmont was also a granddaughter of Governor Desha and a grandniece of Commodore Barney. The cognomens Suffern and Tailer also call up proud lineages. The Tailers emanate from Sir William Tailer, Lieutenant-Governor of Nova Scotia in the Colonial era, who married a niece of Governor Stoughton. The Sufferns were a Huguenot family dating back to Admiral de Suffern under Louis XIV. and whose statue adorns the façade of the Palace of Versailles. Mr. T. Suffern Tailer, Mrs. Sidney J. Smith, Mrs. Robert R. Livingston and Mrs. Henry Lawrence Burnett *née* Agnes Suffern Tailer, all children of Mr. and Mrs. E. N. Tailer *née* Suffern, belong to this noted pedigree. General Burnett, a great-great-grandson of Lieutenant-Governor Burnett, of New Jersey, came from the original Scotch clan which the Robber Barons of Scotland headed centuries ago.

Mr. Lorillard Spencer's mother was a Griswold, a member of one of the greatest Colonial families of the Republic—the Griswolds of Connecticut, a concatenation of celebrities, including more than a dozen governors and thirty-five chief justices. Mrs. James P. Kernochan's mother was also a Griswold of the same illustrious lineage. Mrs. Kernochan's great-grandfather, Colonel Lashar, of New York City, won distinction as a Revolutionary hero. The Princess Cenci, of Rome, is related to Mrs. Kernochan and Mr. Lorillard Spencer. The Spencers were old-time metropolitan society leaders, in direct line from Governor De Witt Clinton and lived for generations in Washington Square. Mrs. Lorillard Spencer is a daughter of Mrs. Charles H. Berryman, who was a Miss Whitney, of New York City, a member of the Stephen Whitney family, and connected with the Phoenix and Suydams, and other people of note; in fact, no other Whitney family in the United States can be mentioned in the same old-time patrician category with the Whitneys of Bowling Green, New York City, where the family occupied an imposing mansion for generations. Of the Stephen Whitney posterity, Mrs. Lorillard Spencer is a beauty of international repute, and a portrait of her taken with one of her children in her arms, has been copied and reproduced as an ideal type in almost every State and territory of the great Republic. The advent into society of her son, Lorillard Spencer III., is adding a renewed zest to Mrs. Spencer's flagging interest of late years in its gayeties.

Mrs. Van Rensselaer Cruger, the first lady of Washington, formerly for many years a leader in the most exclusive coterie of the metropolis, can claim the two royal Governors Wentworth and Lady Elizabeth Wentworth in a direct line back, and is also a grandniece of Washington Irving. Her mother was a Miss Paris, of a family of courtly traditions and social importance; in fact, compared with Mrs. Van Rensselaer Cruger, most other Washington women, whether related to official life or permanent residents, are, in birth, manners and social experience, mere *bourgeoisie*.

The name and fame of old Governor Peter Stuyvesant adds lustre to the pedigrees of Mrs. George W. Vanderbilt, Stuyvesant Fish, Mrs. John Nicholas Brown, Stuyvesant Le Roy, Winthrop Rutherfurd, Rutherfurd Stuyvesant and Mrs. George Grenville Merrill *née* Dresser.

The Goulds of Fairfield, Fairfield County, Connecticut, the ancestors of George Jay Gould, formed in both the early and late Colonial eras one of the most eminent and aristocratic clans in New England. The Goulds were not only rich and important in England, but the pioneer of the Jay Gould branch in this country was the richest man in the Fairfield Colony and his son became Deputy-Governor of Connecticut, to say nothing of the renowned military heroes and statesmen of the Gould family in its earlier and later generations. George Jay

Gould's forefathers were allied to such families as Governor Talcott's, Sir Richard Ward's, Sir Richard Gunville's and the Aaron Burrs and Roger Shermans. Besides Mr. George Jay Gould, Mr. L. F. Holbrook Betts, Oliver Gould Jennings, Spencer Trask, General Joseph Wheeler, Mrs. James Griswold Wentz, Morris K. Jessup, Henry G. Marquand, Dr. George Taylor Stewart, George Foster Peabody, Rev. Edward Everett Hale, and Baroness Elizabeth Schönberg, of Austria, the Countess Castellane, of Paris, and Lady Francis Evans, of England, are all lineal descendants of Andrew Ward, the Connecticut Colonial statesman, son of Sir Richard Ward and grandson of Sir Richard Gunville, from whom Oliver De Lancey Ward and the rest of the Wards of Ward's Island emanated.

How few American families can trace the origin of their pioneer in this country to be that of a son of an English nobleman! In more than eight out of a dozen instances a chasm yawns between the family in the mother country and the first settler in this, which hundreds and sometimes thousands of dollars expended in genealogical research will not bridge over, the services of even Crozier's Armory proving unavailing.

The Marquise de Talleyrand-Périgord, born Elizabeth Curtis, and her sister, the Princess Ruspoli, belong to the patrician Curtis family, of Murray Hill, New York City, related to the Hoffmans and the Murrays of Murray Hill. The Marquise and the Princess were the daughters of the late Joseph Curtis, Esq., of New York and Paris, a descendant of the ancient and honorable Colonial Curtis family of Stratford, Connecticut. The great-grandfather of the Marquise Talleyrand-Périgord, Joseph Davis Beers, the Wall Street banker, built the Southern New Jersey Railroad and it is on a portion of the Beers estate in New Jersey that Chatsworth, the ultra-fashionable and successful country club, founded by the Marquise de Talleyrand-Périgord and officered by Hon. Levi P. Morton, Mr. John E. Parsons and other men of equal note, is situated. The Marquise de Talleyrand and the Princess Ruspoli are lineal descendants of Thomas Welles, the fourth Colonial Governor of Connecticut.

Mrs. Oscar F. Livingston and Mrs. James Francis Sullivan, the latter of Philadelphia, the wife of one of the Quaker City's regnant financiers, are the two beautiful and *distingué* great-grand-daughters of Benjamin Romaine, a highly-connected and eminent Mayor of New York City; grand-daughters of the Hon. Charles Nichols, former U. S. Minister to The Hague, and daughters of the late Washington Romaine Nichols, a well-known lawyer of the metropolis. Mrs. Livingston and Mrs. Sullivan also can produce a pedigree running back to the Sherman family from which Roger

Sherman, a signer of the Declaration of Independence, of the Remonstrance to the King and of the Constitution of the United States, sprang. The Countess of Craven *née* Bradley Martin, and the Countess Castellane *née* Gould, sprang from this same Sherman stock.

A fashionable bachelor of Mrs. Astor's *entourage*, Mr. James Vanderburg Parker, is a member of the noted old Parker family of Boston, from which he inherited a large share of the fortune which has enabled him to be a lifelong man of leisure. From his mother's side of the house, the Vanderburgs of Albany, Mr. Parker can lay claim to a fine strain of Knickerbocker Dutch lineage.

Mrs. Townsend Burden was a Miss Moale, of Baltimore, of one of the pioneer families of the Monumental City, related to the celebrated Byrds, of Westover, Virginia, and the Poultneys, of whom Mr. Walter de Curzon Poultney, Mrs. Burden's cousin, is rightly designated " the first gentleman of Baltimore."

Sir John Vaughan, the redoubtable Britisher who did active service in this country in the Revolutionary era, was a forefather of Mrs. Henry Siegel *née* Marie Vaughan, and of the Misses Georgine and Dorothy Wilde, all of whom come from straight, clear-cut Anglo-Saxon antecedents. Mrs. Siegel's house in Park Lane during the recent London season was much frequented by members of the British nobility. She is a daughter of the late Judge Vaughan, of Illinois, and a grandniece of Governor William Bebb, of Ohio. Her mother was Miss Isabelle Oliver Peters, a granddaughter of Robert Courtney Peters, Esq., owner of the estates of Lloyd's Forest and Camsey's Chance, of Caroline County, Maryland, and related to the old Peters family of Philadelphia. Mrs. Siegel's daughters, the Misses Georgine and Dorothy Wilde, under the patronage of the Princess de Croy, have been passing a year at the famous Convent at Bruge, socially the most *difficile* of admission on the Continent of Europe.

Mr. Frederic Diodati Thompson, named after his kinsman, Count Diodati of Italy, numbers among his progenitors the Gardiners, of the Manor of Gardiner's Island, and the high-born clan of the Thompsons of Long Island. Mr. Diodati Thompson was knighted by the Sultan of Turkey a few years ago and was the late Mr. Ward McAllister's first lieutenant in his famous charge of the 400.

The handsomest coach for four-in-hand seen at Newport last summer belonged to Mr. Jay Coogan, a descendant of Lord Gordon, who spent some time in this country in the Colonial era, leaving a vast landed estate at Argyll, in the upper section of the State of New York. Mr. Coogan, who is the eldest son of James J. Coogan, of New York and Newport, a former President of Manhattan Borough, New

York City, is also connected on his mother's side of the house with the family of Lady Randolph Churchill, now Mrs. Cornwallis West. Lord Gordon, Mr. Coogan's Colonial forebear, belonged to the Scotch ducal Argyll clan.

The Storm-Livingston estate of New York City, from which the Elbridge T. Gerrys and the Charles F. Hoffmans draw a large share of their wealth, was originally the property of the Misses Storm, the daughters of General Storm, of whom one married Mr. Robert Livingston, the father of Mrs. Elbridge T. Gerry, and the other, Glorvina Rossell Storm, became the wife of Samuel Verplanck Hoffman, the grandfather of Mr. Charles F. Hoffman. Although much has been written of the ancestral " Hoffman estate" of late, Samuel Verplanck Hoffman really had but a drop in the bucket compared with the real estate holdings of his wife, Glorvina Storm, of the Storm-Livingston estate. The progenitor of this branch of Hoffmans in this country was Martinus Hoffman, a military officer—an occupation infinitely to be preferred to that of a number of the Knickerbocker Dutch—market gardening. Mrs. Charles F. Hoffman was a Miss Preston, of the family well known in diplomacy.

Of the members of San Francisco's smartest set who have become allied with New York society, perhaps no one has the royal ancestral backing of Mrs. George Taylor Stewart, who was Miss May

Fargo, of San Francisco, coming in a direct line from both King William of Orange and a long dynasty of Saxon kings. Wolfert Webber, Mrs. Stewart's New York City forefather, was a grandson of William of Orange and a kinsman of Anneke Jans, besides being connected with the Romaine, Van Orden and Van Dusen families. Mrs. Stewart's husband, Dr. George Taylor Stewart, the only son of the late ex-Congressman Thomas E. Stewart and Hariette Allen Taylor, is of distinguished New England ancestry, related to the Marquands, Pells, Jessups, and the Wards of Ward's Island. The Stewart country seat at Bay Shore, Long Island, is built on a portion of the original Nicoll Patent granted by King William.

Mr. Ogden Mills's genealogical chart also forms another notable exception to the usual antecedents of the San Francisco set, running as it does straight back to King Robert Bruce through the marriage of his forefather, Richard Mills, of Westchester, New York, to the daughter of Sergeant Francis Nichols, Colonial proprietor of a vast estate at Stratford, Conn., a grandson of Sir George Bruce and a brother of Sir Richard Nicholls, the first English Governor of New York, who named New York and founded Anglo-Saxon supremacy in that city. The Nicoll family of New York and of the Nicoll Patent of landed estates on Long Island, of which Mr. De Lancey Nicoll is a member, are descended from Matthias Nicolls, Secretary of the Colonial Provinces of New York, who was a cousin of Governor Nicholls. Among the other well-known people, besides Mr. Ogden Mills, who can trace their lineage in a straight line back to King Robert Bruce through Sergeant Francis Nichols, are Chauncey M. Depew, General Joseph Wheeler, Mrs. Oscar F. Livingston, Mrs. James Francis Sullivan, of Philadelphia, Mrs. Spencer Trask, George Livingston Nichols, Mrs. James Griswold Wentz, Acosta Nichols and the Right Reverend William Ford Nichols, D.D., LL.D., Bishop of California, who married Miss Ada Quintard, a niece of the late Bishop Quintard. A dynasty of other crowned heads, in addition, forms part of the imperial ægis of General Joseph Wheeler's ancestral dignity.

Charlotte Corday's pictures in the Louvre might almost pass for a likeness of Miss Louise Ward McAllister's grandmother McAllister, the resemblance being due to the fact that Mrs. McAllister was descended on the maternal side from the Corday family of France. Mrs. McAllister *née* Ward, who was the mother of the late Mr. Ward McAllister, was a great-great-granddaughter of the Rev. Gabriel Marion, the grandfather of General Francis Marion. The Rev. Gabriel Marion was the proprietor of an extensive plantation near Charleston, South Carolina. The Wards of the banking firm of Prime, Ward & King formed part of the very van of the old guard of metropolitan society and did honor to the memory of their forefathers, the Governors Ward of Rhode Island.

Of unsurpassed metropolitan lineages, that of Mrs. Frederic Bronson and Mrs. Lloyd C. Griscom *née* Elsa Bronson, who was one of the bridesmaids of the Duchess of Marlborough, includes Lady Kitty Duer, Lord Stirling, Hon. Rufus King, Archibald Gracie and a galaxy of other celebrities and social leaders. Mrs. Bronson was Miss Sara Gracie King, a daughter of the late Archibald Gracie King, and was ranked one of the most aristocratic belles of the metropolis. The Gracie mansion, where King Louis Phillipe and Lafayette were entertained, the summer home of her great grandfather, Archibald Gracie, Esq., still stands in East River Park, fronting Hell Gate, the former scene of probably the most sumptuous entertaining in the annals of old New York Society, as its spacious banqueting hall alone would partially attest.

The late Mr. Frederic Bronson's mother was a Brinkerhoff and he was also related to the Egerton L. Winthrop and Hollis H. Hunnewell families. Mr. Bronson was for years president of the Metropolitan Coaching Club, and the house parties at his country seat, Verna House, built Italian villa style, on Greenfield Hill, Fairfield, Connecticut, were justly accounted the most fashionable and *distingué* of any given in the State of Connecticut. Miss Elsa

Bronson, the only daughter of Mrs. Frederic Bronson, married Mr. Lloyd C. Griscom, U. S. Minister to Japan, a son of Clement C. Griscom, of Philadelphia.

The proud race of Baltimoreans to which Mr. Harper Pennington can claim the honor of belonging is closely related to the great ducal house of Leeds: his mother was grandniece of a Duchess of Leeds. The Carrolls of Carrollton and the famous McTavish belles of Baltimore are also kinsfolk of Mr. Harper Pennington and so were the three Caton beauties, known as the "Three American Graces" at the court of George III.

The rise of the Colonial and patriotic organizations has given a decided impetus to the fostering of family traditions and lineages even among ultrafashionable folk. And the work of these organizations in cherishing the sentiment of patriotism and preserving the landmarks of American history, cannot be too highly commended in this era of excessive European immigration to our shores and when persons of pure and unadulterated American and English descent are so rapidly disappearing from our United States census. Mrs. Donald McLean, who is the regent of the banner chapter of Daughters of the American Revolution—the New York City chapter—is doing through her own efforts, coupled with those of her chapter, a noble and monumental work for promoting patriotic education and knowledge of the history of our country among all classes, and I know of no other woman so eminently fitted for the office of President-General of the National Society of Daughters of the American Revolution, which will ultimately be hers if justice and equity prevail.

Almost on the edge of the crown land of Windsor Forest, Windsor Castle, England, stands a light yellow-colored mansion, New Lodge, Windsor Forest, the country seat of Queen Victoria's favorite godson, at whose christening she was personally present—Lieut.-Colonel Victor Bates Van de Meyer, who married Lady Emily Georgiana, a daughter af the late Earl of Craven, a sister of Lady Coventry and aunt of the young Earl of Craven, who married Miss Bradley Martin. The Van de Weyer town house stands in Arlington Street, S. W., between Lord Wimborne's and Lord Salisbury's.

Lieut.-Colonel Van de Weyer's grandfather, Joshua Bates, the London banker, was an American. Lieut.-Colonel Van de Weyer is related to Mr. George Foster Peabody, the banker-philanthropist of New York, who is descended from Andrew Ward, the Connecticut statesman, the Marquis of Chamilly and Marshall of France, the Nicholses of Nichols and the Burroughs of Bridgeport. At the old Burroughs family mansion, once a spacious landmark of this latter city, Joshua Bates was a frequent guest of his brother-in-law, Stephen Bur-

71

roughs III., the son of Stephen Burroughs II., the inventor of the decimal system of notation. Mr. Walter Burroughs Nichols, of Bridgeport, formerly of New York City, who married his cousin, a Miss Nichols of Nichols, is the nearest relation Lieut.-Colonel Van de Weyer, of Windsor Forest, Queen Victoria's godson, has living in this country.

Joshua Bates, Lieut.-Colonel Van de Weyer's grandfather, from whom he inherited New Lodge. Windsor Forest, married Lucretia Jennings, a daughter of Levi Jennings, of Boston, formerly of Fairfield, Conn., and of the same family as Mr. Oliver Gould Jennings, of New York and Newport, who has an eseate with a Colonial mansion at Fairfield, Conn. Mrs. Oliver Gould Jennings', *née* Brewster, lineage can be traced to the Mayflower pioneer bearing the same patronymic.

In conclusion, a general hubbub about coats-of-arms has lately been stirred up among the ultra-smart, who are greatly addicted to the use of armorial bearings, by an Englishman, William Armstrong Crozier, F.R.S., now resident in New York City, and backed by the Royal College of Arms, of London. Crozier's General Armory has leaped into fame as an arbiter on what American families are entitled to bear arms and what are remanded to have their armorial bearings scraped off from their carriage doors *instanter!*

CHAPTER VI.

Equipage, Style of Living and Entertaining.

THE ultra-smart definition of poverty is having only one man-servant in one's house. For such a simple act of courtesy as serving a cup of five o'clock tea to a solitary visitor there must be two men-servants in attendance—one to open the door and the other to bring in the tea things.

An ideally complete establishment employs besides a chef, a cook and kitchen maid, a second kitchen maid, known as a scullery, one or two laundresses, a parlor maid and three or four men, viz.: a butler, second man, third man and fourth man. The third man does dining-room work and valeting, the fourth useful work, like cleaning. Mrs. Vanderbilt, Mr. and Mrs. William K. Vanderbilt, Mr. and Mrs. Andrew Carnegie, Mr. and Mrs. George Jay Gould and the Whitelaw Reids are especially noteworthy for the retinue of servants in their establishments.

But consider a few of the other accessories of state and equipage. Such a *ménage* is expected to be supplied with about the following cavalcade of turnouts: an omnibus, more commonly called an opera 'bus; a mail coach and brake for four-in-hand driving, a victoria, a spider phaeton, a runabout, station wagon, a mail phaeton for men's driving, a one-horse cabriolet, a two-wheel gig, besides a basket phaeton for young women. To the New York City stable of the family, in the season, we will add a bachelor's brougham for one horse, another two-horse brougham for women and a hansom cab. Such an equipped stable requires from six to ten horses and the services of half a dozen or more men.

Mrs. Stuyvesant Fish, a practical horsewoman in a quiet way, who is seen sometimes over at the mart in East Twenty-fourth Street buying a horse, usually has her brougham taken with her to Newport, at variance with the general custom in this respect. Maroon is Mrs. Fish's favorite color for her carriages, Mr. John Sloane's is green; the colors of the Vanderbilts, William Douglass Sloanes and Twombleys are maroon and canary; blue is the color of Messrs. Clarence H. Mackay and Charles Lanier ; magenta and green of Edward R. Thomas.

Quiet, sober tones in the painting and decorations of carriages obtain to a great extent also among the other real ultra-fashionables. With the upper West Side plutocrats of the metropolis, on the other hand, the colors of the rainbow lend themselves with prodigal hand for variegating broughams, cabriolets, victorias or almost any old thing on wheels. Pathetic it is that it cannot be drilled into some of these people that a coat-of-arms—provided it be honestly acquired—should not be blazoned on any smaller vehicle than a big landau or the largest size of brougham. It is, moreover, useless to tell a few of the more flashy of these individuals that if on heraldry bent, their *crests* should be used on their cabriolets, victorias and small broughams, for the simple reason that they cannot distinguish between a coat-of-arms and a crest.

Anent of quiet, sober tones in colors for vehicles, Mr. Jay Coogan's four-in-hand coach, which won so many plaudits at Newport, made to order by a Paris firm, was painted at his special suggestion a very dark shade of green and black, with white enamel used for the panelling of the doors. Mr. Coogan had a string of fifteen· horses at the stables of White Hall, his father's villa, one of the show places of Newport, his pair of polo ponies distancing almost any of the others brought to the polo-loving City by the Sea.

Then, to add to the regal state of fashionable rapid transit, there are the private cars and whole trains *de luxe*—Mr. J. Pierpont Morgan's favorite way of entertaining, the great churchman-financier seldom being so happy as when scurrying across the continent aboard one of these palaces on wheels filled with bishops as his guests. So minutely does

Mr. Morgan minister to the welfare and comfort of these itinerating ecclesiastics that he never fails to have his physician comprised in the party.

The keeping of a yacht is no more *en règle* for a fashionable family than that a *gentleman nowadays* should be college-bred.

About one's mode of living, the palatial family hotel, a twentieth century marvel of comfort and luxury, ridding one of the vexed servant problem, will have a growing tendency to compete with the town house as a winter residence during the brief and broken-up season in town. Mr. and Mrs. Alfred G. Vanderbilt occupied an apartment in a family hotel last winter. Of these hostelries, the new St. Regis, in Fifth Avenue, is voted the handsomest and most commodious in the world, its royal suite of apartments, consisting of only five rooms, occupied lately by that prince of entertainers, Mr. Edward R. Thomas, commanding a rental of forty-five thousand dollars a year.

Elegant simplicity is the keynote to Mrs. Astor's style of entertaining. Born a Knickerbocker, she has an innate shrinking from the seeming vulgarity of great wealth, although recognizing its necessity for carrying on society. And she always has mixed in with the multi-millionaires, at her state dinners and balls, personages the amount of whose goods and chattels would draw no satellites about them. Mrs. Astor, contrary to the popular myths, is not

a woman who thinks in " 150s," " 400s " or " 600s,"
the talismanic " 600 " chancing to be nearer than
some other number to that of the guest-list of her
annual ball. She is, above all, a *practical* social
leader and not given to airing theories of caste or
evolving Hellenic unities. She goes out in society
now only to a moderate degree and is withdrawing
more from its gayeties.

Gifted with marvellous social talent, which always includes tact and diplomacy, well born, of
more than passing personal comeliness and grace
of manner, Mrs. Astor rose to the leadership of
American society by the acclamation of society itself. Still, one must not be unmindful that when
Mr. Ward McAllister adjudged in her favor the
question of precedence between the two Mrs. Astors
as to which should be Mrs. Astor *assoluta* and also
ruled that, counter to the claims of a powerful
rival, she should be assigned the place of first lady
at the great Centennial ball in New York, all
this was not without its effects. Mr. McAllister
at that time was in the effulgence of his power
as a social dictator, although his dictatorship subsequently waned, owing to internecine jealousies
and rival claims of the new millionaires.

Mr. Elisha Dyer, Jr., a man man of extraordinary tact and diplomacy, of good, sound business
judgment, never talking for publication, steering
clear of the spectacular, and democratic, and genial

to a degree to meet socially, is looked up to by the men and women of the "magic circle" as its male Coryphæus.

Of the elaborate and eminently picturesque type of entertaining, Mrs. Cornelius Vanderbilt, Jr., Mrs. Hermann Oelrichs, Mrs. Oliver H. P. Belmont, Mrs. Clarence H. Mackay, Mrs. George Jay Gould and Mrs. Stuyvesant Fish may be cited as exponents. Mrs. Oelrichs's *bal blanc* at Rosecliff, her Newport villa, will go down into social history for a long time to come. She and Mrs. William K. Vanderbilt, Jr., have evidently inherited the artistic trend of their mother, the wife of the late U. S. Senator Fair, of San Francisco, whose dinners and balls were given on a scale of Oriental magnificence. The California '49ers, the Fairs, Floods, Hearsts, Crockers, D. Ogden Millses, Mackays and their peers, at a time, too, when multi-millionaires of equal fortune were somewhat scarce in New York City, made up their minds that no matter how short some their pedigrees were, they themselves would live well and long. Accordingly they they set themselves to work to invent the art of dining. And Mr. Ward McAllister, during his stay in San Francisco as a young man, acquired the whole gastronomic art of war of the '49ers and came back and imparted what he knew to benighted New York, then in the throes of the mincing and pinched-up Knickerbocker régime.

Mr. McAllister's forerunner in this epicurean mission to New York was his uncle, Sam Ward, who married a Miss Astor, a sister of the late William Astor, and was the brother of the severely ethical, handsome, courtly and severely intellectual Mrs. Julia Ward Howe.

THE SOCIETY OF THE FUTURE

In casting the horoscope of the society of the future, the claims of genius and cleverness will be more fully recognized by the Golden Caste of Vere de Vere; the author, the musical virtuoso, the journalist and the actor enjoying equal precedence with the society portrait painter at the tables of the social oligarchs. But some of the men and women of talent and cleverness, on their part, will have to be less enterprising about trying to work off their schemes on their multi-millionaire hosts and hostesses, and will need to stand in somewhat more respectful awe of them, in this respect, just as gifted English guests do of their nobles, not regarding them in the cold, calculating light of utility men and women.

Society at present is in its golden age in not much more than one sense, but the good leaven is working, and that of the still somewhat remote future will not rest content to be penned up in a coterie made up largely of the ephemeral plutocracy of the hour, where a family is wealthy, and to the fore one year and the next drops out of sight. Among the younger social oligarchs, the seer discerns two born leaders—Mrs. Cornelius Vanderbilt, Jr., and Mrs. Clarence H. Mackay. Wedded, too, as the former is to a man of genius, we may also look to that quarter for a broadening out of social conditions. Mrs. Clarence H. Mackay, born a Duer, and grand daughter of the wit, William R. Travers, is eminently fitted to head a *salon*. Mrs. Mackay received with Mrs. Patrick Campbell, the actress, on the stage of the theatre at a matinée, after the play, and often mixes in people of talent and *esprit* with those of the Golden Caste of Vere de Vere around her festive board, thus trying to temper the undue afflatus of wealth. Mrs. John Jacob Astor and Mrs. Ogden Mills, both also patricians to their finger tips, will always help to guide the social destinies of state.

We are growing every day more cosmopolitan, and I see, in the society of the future, a circle of brilliants, if one may be allowed the figure, radiant with the good sense of the countrymen of Locke, and Bacon, the wit and epigrammatic brilliancy of the clear-cut compatriots of Montaigne, and the depth of the land of mystic philosophy and dreams.

CHAPTER VII.

MARRIAGE outright into the smart set is far and away the surest method of effecting an entrance into it; few visiting lists, for example, having undergone a more radical change than that of Mrs. Drexel-Dahlgren since her marriage to Mr. Harry Lehr. Another expeditious method is by means of a business deal, benefiting one or more members of the smart set—not a hard cash bargaining for social promotion, although men have been known to form business partnerships for this express object; but, to illustrate—a short time ago a railroad transaction secured admission for a family into an influential section of the "magic circle." There are delicate ways of conveying the expression of one's social needs, and the ultra-smart are endowed with a fine sense of *noblesse oblige*, provided one is manipulating events so as to fill their purses.

An annually increasing quota of candidates for metropolitan social honors, or rather, adoption, is made up of rich—suddenly rich western people. Such a family, we will premise, is about to estab-

itself in a New York town house. If you are socially ambitious, do not set up your domicile on the upper West Side, but fix your abode as near as possible to "Millionaires' Row," the Fifth avenue court end of Central Park—not necessarily an unduly ostentatious house which will egg everyone on to asking the dread question, "Who is who?" but letting the show-place come a few years later, after you are well placed socially. A grandiose house on a conspicuous thoroughfare, with no suitable guests to fill it, like the gigantic edifices of the Bank of Italy and Ministry of Finance in Rome, is an exclamation point strongly provocative of irony.

Your household gods suitably enshrined, employ a press agent at once, but be wary of too much publicity, for in the main, the rôle of inglorious obscurity is the one you will need to play, until you know the ropes better. At the same time you can afford to pay the press agent well for having it inserted in the personal columns of a big daily which caters to fashionable folk, that you sail for Europe on such a date, or have returned from your country house for the season; so that, at least, you will not be hampered by persons protesting, "I have never heard of those people."

A particular phase of newspaper publicity to fight shy of is that involved in allowing the women of your family to become enrolled as members of certain clubs and charities, and having their names bundled out in the third-class society column of a certain Sunday paper with lists of "detrimentals"* of the first water, numbers of them turning out to be veritable mill-stones hung about the neck of social aspiration. A woman of fashion and a club-woman are two mutually excluding entities—two totally distinct creations of Almighty God, although the latter often tries to palm herself off as the former.

If your early training in drawing-room deportment has been defective or wholly lacking—and as likely as not it has—place yourself at once under such a social mentor as Miss d'Angelo Bergh, the leader of the metropolitan musical smart set. Have her put the society intonation for a speaking voice into your throat, teach you easy deportment and carriage, how to enter and leave a drawing-room, how to converse with the latest society badinage, and how to give a musicale. To illustrate these points from the ranks of highest fashion: Few society women have been as close students of Delsarte as Mrs. Burke-Roche.

A scion of the Ducal house of Russell and also of the d'Angelo nobility, related to the Charles H. Marshalls and to the patrician Morse family of this city, besides the Wrights, Morses and Russells of

*A "detrimental" is a technical social term and means a person of however excellent moral character or ability, who does not blend well *socially* with either the conservative Knickerbocker element or the Ultra fashionables.

Boston, Miss d'Angelo Bergh has been presented at several European courts, decorated by France, and is a prodigy of cultivation.

The American aptitude *par excellence* is our facility for seizing an opportunity. As Americans, our manners are our weak point, and the sooner we rid ourselves of all foolish self-consciousness on this point, and bow down to this humiliating fact, the sooner shall we mend our ways and stand on a more equal social footing with older forms of civilization than our own, and, above all, with the best bred people of our own country, to whose companionship we aspire. The old saying that it takes two generations to make a gentleman is being refuted every day, for Americans are remarked not only for their facility in amassing fortunes, but in furnishing themselves with presentable manners on short notice, under the right environment, and under proper mentors.

The next move for the social aspirant will be to cultivate the acquaintance of some fashionable woman whose finances are on the wane, but whose temperament requires the expenditure of large sums of money, and who is, moreover, a walking American De Brett and Burke, in short, a running commentary as to knowing who are the people one can receive. Conceding that introductions may be very sparingly given, her help will, in a negative way, be of much value in warding off "detrimentals," thus saving you years of undoing and weeding out.

When one pauses to reflect upon the vast fund of energy, time and money annually expended in New York City by social aspirants in entertaining the wrong people—people who are positive dragons besetting the pathway of social progress, these foregoing monitions cannot be too often reiterated.

Form the acquaintance of an occasional visiting nobleman, if fully assured he is not an imposter, and that he is received by persons who might be made, possibly, to fall in line some way for furthering your campaigns. Minister well to his gastronomic needs, for in all probability, he has taken lodgings *sans* meals. But avoid making yourself unduly conspicuous in public print with these people of title, for should any one of them turn out to be a scapegrace, the satirical periodicals will show you up as a nobody caught in the *flagrante delictu* of snobbishness and hanging on by the eyebrows. If, on the other hand, a titled European is comfortably wealthy and *persona grata* at the houses of the highest fashion, do not waste much time and effort over him, for in all probability he will front you as soon as he has ascertained your exact social status. With reference to your own countrymen all along, give a wide berth to certain *soi disant* society folk of the upper West Side, who will get your name in the newspapers morning, noon and night and three times on Sunday, until it becomes case-hardened on the lists of the socially impossible.

The snubs, cuffs and slings of outrageous fortune you are experiencing on every hand, may be perverting you into a woman hater and a cynic when your youth and beauty are at their zenith; but keep up a bold front, steering clear of flamboyant toilettes, for a woman needs to be astonishingly well placed socially to dress like a cocotte.

And, above all, be philanthropic with your purse, although, perchance, the heart responds but feebly. Conditions have changed a good deal since William D. Howells wrote his "Traveler in Altruria," and fashionable charities as an adjuvant to social climbing are growing more difficult to be worked, and the Church still more intractable for these ends; but there is a *dernier ressort;* join the Countess Leary's charities. No matter if you are a Calvinistic Presbyterian of bilious hue, or a transcendental Unitarian of diaphanous pallor, and she wishes you to donate, and take active part in an entertainment to found a college for the avowed purpose of preventing Roman Catholics from entering Protestant colleges. No matter if the management will not deign to have your name appear on the printed patroness list, calling you a "patroness" when no one besides yourself is within hearing distance; invest in a stout package of tickets at five dollars each. People of the same Protestant persuasion as yourself have done this self-same thing, with good rate of interest accruing in rise of social values, and the percents. are annually increasing.

The Episcopal church and the Catholic church are the churches of beautiful manners, and if your birth has placed you under the social ban of being a dissenter, cultivate Episcopal emotions and shuffle off the mortal coil of Presbyterianism on as short notice as possible. Ralph Waldo Emerson, in his "English Traits," said no truer thing than "You can tell a dissenter by his manners." You can divine that some women were not born in the Church by their smile. Beware, then, of sectarian smiles —those unmeaning smiles, such as the wife of a certain General of the United States army and her daughter, who subsequently became a princess, lavished so *de trop* on Newport cottagers the first season after Mrs. Astor's house-warming, when they visited the wife of an hotel keeper at her Newport villa, and introduced their hostess right and left.

If you are blessed with young daughters, no matter what your creed, hurry them away to a French convent; for a convent is a school of respect, a nursery of beautiful manners, inculcating what always makes a young woman doubly attractive to mankind—the subjection of women. To see convent-bred manners in their full flower and fruition, one really needs to know the delightful society of Continental Europe.

Do not, I beg of you, make a national one-night stand theatre comique of yourself and family by making the grand tour of hiring cottages at Newport, Lenox and the other ultra-smart resorts before society has given the slightest recognition to your claims. Invoke the aid of old Father Neptune; secure a yacht, as sumptuous a one as you please, and, socially speaking, if your bark sink, 'tis to another sea. If ignored or snubbed at Newport, spread sail for Narragansett Pier or Bar Harbor, felicitating yourself that the social thud is not barbed with the added poignancy of one's having been a cottager in a place and not being received. Besides, there is no more acceptable way of entertaining and of putting people under heavy social obligations to one than by giving yachting parties. The rapid social headway a certain family from the West is, at the present hour, making with our social oligarchs is due partly to the fact that the ultra-smart women who are going social sponsor for them cannot afford to keep a yacht.

During this your period of social probation go to Europe rather often in your yacht. If you cannot master the art of war of the ultra-smart at home, study it abroad, but do not suffer yourself to be deluded into the belief that the entree into America's exclusive set is to be secured through European social alliances or meeting fashionable Americans abroad. All such finessing, like forming ocean steamship acquaintances, is a thing of the past; but contact with the great world of Europe will ennoble your manners, imparting an air of distinction and greater confidence in approaching the *fin fleur* of your own countrymen's society.

Go abroad early and stay late, in the London season, stopping at the Carlton or at Claridge's, at all events, dining and supping frequently at the Carlton. Secure the services of a high-class social promoter; such a person can be corralled by judicious advertising from the ranks of the nobility for a sufficient price. Only a short time ago an English woman, backed by an eminent peeress, guaranteed to several Americans court presentations to Edward himself at five thousand dollars a head! Arrange with the promoter to have a dinner given in your name at the Carlton in honor of a distinguished peer or peeress, with covers laid for no other Americans besides yourselves, and see that the event is given the widest possible exploiting on both sides of the Atlantic. If, during your European sojourns, you fall in with fashionable Americans, try, by delicate and becoming advances, to ingratiate yourself with them, leaving it entirely to them, however, to take the initiative of keeping up the acquaintance on American soil. Strenuously avoid even the semblance of future building upon them, or banking on the name after your return home.

Should it finally be your good fortune to receive an invitation to the church for a wedding in a really fashionable family, for which invitations have been sent out by the thousands, make a costly and artistic present. More than likely it will receive mention in the newspapers through the kind offices of society reporters, whom your husband has treated to champagne galore, and one or two of whom have perhaps shown their gallantry by inserting your name in their columns among lists of guests at smart entertainments, at which you were neither present in the body nor honored with an invitation. At all events, the general public, which is hot-headed, upon reading of your extravagant wedding gift, will jump to the conclusion that you were, of course, bidden to the reception. Provided the marriage is not altogether a cold-blooded one of convenience, a feeling toward yourself closely simulating gratitude may well up in the hearts of the bride and her family.

This clever little stratagem was resorted to by an aspiring family of wealthy Newport cottagers invited to the church for the Oelrichs-Martin wedding, and to this day is yielding a good bonus in social returns. It is also sometimes practiced by a finessing member of the Newport cottage colony, the daughter of an old-time shop-keeper of one of the most plebeian trades, whose social position is on the wane, and who, having pretty much relinquished hopes of being invited to most of the ultra-smart dinners—being even willing to have personages from that coterie urged to come to her cottage as dinner guests, without a return in kind, is putting up a hard fight to keep in evidence at least for the balls and general entertainments.

As to the art of entertaining during this the trying-on time of your social reincarnation, you must accept with true Christian resignation the truth of the major promise that you yourself are not worth meeting, and accordingly, as many of your dinners and musicales as possible—you are to give musicales instead of receptions—must have as a social *pièce de resistance* a guest of honor. And as it will be an affront to the guest of honor, if those of her friends bidden do not grace your house with their presence, there you are, with a number of smart people meshed in the toils of a very effectual form of polite coercion. The guest of honor subterfuge works equally well for a family which has held high position and is on the down grade socially. A débutante or lately betrothed young girl is the most suitable and unsuspecting guest of honor to subserve such an end.

Sedulously avoid sending out cards for general reception days for the season, or for a series of any length, of informal afternoons at home with music, for undesirable persons and social mountebanks are sure to take undue advantage of such loop holes.

Be at home on Sunday afternoons at five o'clock, to serve tea, but issue no cards to that effect, having it given out that those of your friends whom you really desire to have come are bidden by verbal invitation, and that you receive only a few. It is, of course, taken for granted that you have been all along a close student of fashionable society and have perceived that there are only two sets in society with which a really ambitious person should have anything to do—the smart set and its outer fringe, and the old Knickerbocker and Colonial families. I speak advisedly of the latter, for should one finally not succeed in penetrating into the true ultra-smart inner circle, the defeat can be partially cloaked by falling back upon the Knickerbockers. And their names at every stadium of the upward climb will pose well in the newspapers with those of the few rather smart guests whom you, perchance, may be able to muster for your dinners and musicales. In general, whenever you receive a social thud from an ultra-fashionable, fly into the arms of a Knickerbocker.

Among Knickerbockers and Colonials there are varying degrees of fashionable validity, and I append herewith a partial list of those standing nearest the throne of ultra-smartness as an ideal goal to be aspired to, although in all probability, you will have to rest content with the companionship of much lesser lights of the Knickerbocker peerage around your festive board. Bear in mind that those Knickerbockers whom I check off in what follows, are all refined and honored citizens, but simply can not be classed as ultra-fashionable, or as standing in as close proximity to the smartest set as some others, as likely as not thinking the ultra-smart game not worth the candle.

Of Van Rensselaers, the Alexander Ran Rensselaers of *New York*, to whom Mrs. Edmund L. Baylies, Miss Alice Van Rensselaer and Mrs. Van Rensselaer-Johnson belong, are of premier importance. The Philadelphia Alexander Van Rensselaers are not especially given to desiccating social flavors, and ranging themselves in line with the new Golden Caste of Vere de Vere.

Do not be hypnotized by the name, then, and if a Van Rensselaer be inclined to be overbearing, quietly remind him that the first Van Rensselaer Patroon was a tradesman when he came to this country. For the purpose you have in hand, accordingly, separate carefully the Van Rensselaer chaff from the Van Rensselaer wheat.

Then there are the Oakley and Philip Rhinelanders, the only ultra-fashionable Rhinelanders; the Sir Frederic J. de Peysters, who are not the Fourteenth Street de Peysters; the Kips and the Gardiners of the manor of Gardiner's Island; the Livingston Beeckmans, Duers, the various Winthrop families, especially the Egerton L. and Buchanan

Winthrops, and the E. N. Tailers; these will all be helpful, provided you can only get the presentation, which is not easy. Of Livingstons, the Goodhue, Maturin, Johnston and Oscar Livingstons are rather to be preferred. Of Hoffmans, the Charles F. and Francis Burrall Hoffmans and William M. V. Hoffmans are far and away the most fashionable. If you cannot deal with these, the principals, angle for their relations. Study the doings of society closely and which Knickerbockers are enjoying any fashionable vogue or lead up to any, will be readily apparent. Be wary and sly about it, but be willing to invest hundreds of dollars if need be in having every nook and cranny of your own and your husband's pedigrees searched, and if you should light upon any presentable ancestry, you could confide the find as old-time history, known for generations by your family, to an occasional Knickerbocker acquaintance; but I beg of you, do not go to the extreme of hanging the walls of your dining-room with counterfeit presentments of assumed " ancestors." Also, do not unmuzzle yourself on the forefather claim to any member of the smart set, unless desirous of being made a laughing-stock. In general, few conversational *faux pas* lay bare one's *bourgeoisie* social origin more glaringly than talking of one's lineage on short acquaintance with a person, or under any circumstances with an Englishman to whom all Americans alike are commoners.

Aim at originality and the freshest European modes in your style of entertaining, and do not omit your prayers to old Father Neptune. For instance, if your winter's social campaign warrants your leasing a cottage at Newport, put your yacht in commission and have it given out that although you have hired a sumptuous villa, you are so much of a sea-dog that you are going to live on your yacht more than half of the time. If dinner invitations do not come pouring in as fast as you like, take frequent little cruises of a day or two on your yacht, having mention made in the newspapers by your publicity agent every time you get on or off your aquatic social motor. These pretty manœuvres on land and sea were successfully gone through this last season at the City by the Sea by a family of aspirants, reinforced by a triple alliance of social luminaries, with a brilliant and spectacular social leader pitted against the campaign.

Suffer the horse, too, to help you along up the social hill of difficulty. Invest in a string of race-horses and be an exhibitor at the various fashionable horse shows, provided yourself or your husband have a genuine and unaffected love of the horse. See what wonders the equine god has wrought for the Edward R. Thomases and the Thomas Hastings in a social way. Contrast the list of guests bidden to the Presbyterian church at Greenwich only two or three years ago, to the wedding of Mr.

and Mrs. Thomas Hastings *née* Benedict, with the ultra-smart coterie in which they are to-day moving, Mrs. Hastings now queening it as president of a coaching club, composed of a whole section of the most fashionable horsewomen in America!

In fine, it is but a truism to reflect that the rôle of whole groups of those now high and mighty in the national smart set has been essentially that of climbers. Not many years ago the family of a leading metropolitan physician, people well placed socially, sent out cards for a débutante's reception for their handsome daughter. "Now I give you *carte blanche* for flowers, music, caterers and everything else to make Clara's début a notable one, but I have one favor to beg and I must be peremptory about it, *pater familias* insisted—the So and So's must be invited."

"Impossible!" his aristocratic wife threw up her hands. "Those girls dress abominably, and the man is so untutored, he can't even pronounce Fifth avenue; he calls it 'Fit' avenue.'"

"But he is a very lucrative patient of mine and he came around to my office this morning and told me he had read the notice of our reception in the *Tribune*, and that his one ambition in life was for his family to get into society. And besides, you will give his wife the credit of doing a thinking part of doing no talking at all. If a woman doesn't open her mouth, she certainly does not expose her crudity."

They were invited. Two of those "abominably dressed girls" are at the present hour queening it not only in American, but in international society, one of them being the mother of a duchess, both allied by marriage to colossal fortunes of world-wide prestige, and both playing the hostess aboard their own yachts, and at their own sweet will, to the crowned heads of Europe!

Parnassus widens, as we leave the summit.

CHAPTER VIII.

The Misadventures of Mrs. Detrimental—A Social Career.

RS. DETRIMENTAL, a sort of female knight errant of social adventure—a somewhat prevalent type. Birthplace, Denver—a propitious social star to be born under. Father, a livery-stable keeper—not so lucky an omen. Paternal grandfather, cook for miners' camps—not a bar sinistre in Denver society. Mrs. Detrimental's mother, however, with only a country district primary school training, secures a good education for her pretty daughter, who eventually marries a crude, rough-and-ready multi-millionaire, controlling mines eclipsing the wealth of Ormus or Ind.

The Detrimentals start out from Denver.

As for society, Mr. Detrimental "wants none of it," but shares heart and soul, as a silent partner, his wife and daughter's unquenchable ambitions. Mrs. Detrimental and her daughter accordingly betake themselves to the metropolis for a couple of winters, establishing themselves in a showy house on Riverside Drive. They invest heavily in two charities and are soon bidden to dances and lunches by *soi disant* "social leaders" who lie in wait for Western *nouveaux riches*. Alas! by a collision of carriages, the smashing of automobiles, or some other accident, they fall in for a bit with a genuine woman of fashion of the *fin fleur* of the smart set. Mrs. Detrimental confides to her her social campaign projects, quoting with elation and peculiar swelling of the throat as friends the names of Mrs. So-and-So, the aforesaid leaders of the "best society."

The smart woman takes the ground from under Mrs. Detrimental's feet by confronting her with the statement that the alleged "social leaders" quoted by her are themselves "detrimentals." The woman of fashion quickly perceives that personally she can do nothing socially for Mrs. Detrimental but give advice, as a long and tedious technical training is needed, and wisely tells her to pack her trunks for a winter in Rome, this chancing to be an auspicious year—the Anno Santo or Holy Jubilee year. They sail in November, finding to their dismay only one passenger of the real American ultra-fashionable set on board the huge North German Lloyd steamer, and she refuses, not only by actions, but by words, to have anything to do with Mrs. and Miss Detrimental, although she is so hard pressed by *ennui* that she takes up with a pretty female purchasing agent

from Wanamaker's millinery department and her companion, a sleek drummer, even sitting at a small table with them in the dining saloon, as they could levy no sort of social claim upon her.

Shortly before the steamer reaches port the Detrimentals fall in with a young man of stranded exchequer who had lately dropped down and out of the smart set of New York and Newport for that obvious reason. They wisely adopt him for a social cicerone, after proper inquiries, and stop at the Grand Hotel, Rome, by his advice, dining him often, receiving as recompense a few introductions to really smart Americans, who are held back from going down to Egypt for the winter by rumors of the plague. Mrs. Detrimental and her daughter hire a pew in the American Episcopal Church in the Via Nationale and give liberally besides to the rector in aid of the conversion of Catholics to Episcopalians and their own conversion to smartness, following this up with a dinner at the Grand Hotel in honor of the rector, for which he invites two-thirds of the guests. The rector speaks a good word for them to their Ambassador, to whom they brought no letters, and they receive an invitation to a reception of their country's supreme representative at the Piombino Palace, their *point de resistance* on this occasion being, not their manners, which were only tolerable, but their gowns—copies of their North German Lloyd cynosure's.

A nobleman to whom Mrs. Detrimental's secretary had loaned money, *sans* returns, years before secures for them an introduction by means of which they become registered at the Palestra on the Quirinal Hill, Rome's exclusive Casino and Miss Detrimental, who is pretty and *chic*, is actually bidden to join the hunting set of Italian nobility and fashionable Americans scurrying out over the old Appian Way for a steeplechase. The Ambassador, a knowing man of the world, speedily divines the supreme aim and goal of Mrs. Detrimental's existence to be not Rome, Paris or London, but Newport, and accordingly recommends her to secure the entree of the Tuesday receptions given by Hayward, the honorary Papal Chamberlain, at his sumptuous palace near St. Peter's, but offers not a hand to help.

Mrs. Detrimental now buys up, at an exorbitant price, some tickets to the Tribuna, out in the portico of St. Peter's, to range her party in juxtaposition to the Papal and other nobility, to witness the splendid ceremony of the opening of the Holy Door on this the Christmas Eve of the Jubilee year, thus placing a couple of smart Americans under heavy obligations by accepting them. Though themselves Protestant Episcopalians—since the date when Mrs. Detrimental conceived the idea of being born again smart—they now, all of a sudden, exhibit a leaning toward the Church of Rome, at least as long as their conversation with the rector of the American College, who has secured them a presentation to the Pope, lasts, Mrs. Detrimental actually warming up, under the influence of Roman candles, to the extent of offering a donation to be applied to the purchase of rugs to be laid on the cold stone pavements of the students' cells, the upshot of the matter being that some Tuesday the Detrimentals find their feet trending the scarlet velvet carpetings of the courts and grand staircases of Bramante's masterpiece, the Palazzo Giraud, the palace of Honarary Papal Chamberlain Hayward, the social leader of English-Speaking Catholics in Rome, at whose levees a chosen few wealthy American Episcopalians are in attendance. Towards the approach of Mardi Gras, Mrs. Detrimental, at the instigation of her secretary, the social cicerone adverted to, manages to have it leak out that she will donate a princely sum of money to the king, to have the carnival in the Corso restored that year, provided others will combine financial forces—she knows well enough they will not—but Miss Detrimental's dot has become town talk all the same.

But she and her daughter are all the while actually en route for Newport, and already racking their brains to try to conjecture what proportion of those few smart Americans in Rome, whose summer habitat is Newport, and upon whom they are now lavishing money, will not by August be suffering from aphasia and every sort of other queer lapses of tongue and memory. Abandoning the saturnalia of their Roman triumphs at just the proper time, our heroine, her daughter and their suite of courier, French maid, male mentor and coach—now installed secretary at a fixed salary in reality, but made to pose as society man in public —take the train *de luxe* for Paris, quartering themselves at the Hotel Ritz.

The excitement over shopping at Paquin's, Doucet's and the millinery and jewelry shops along the Rue de la Paix acts as a rest-cure for several days, after keeping up an enforced and precarious social position in the Eternal City, but they speedily find that the social triumphs of the Grand Hotel, Rome, are not to be repeated, even on a small scale, at the Ritz. But to her joy, Mrs. Detrimental finally descries on the hotel register of the Paris edition of the New York *Herald* the name of an American family of fashion whom she had entertained once at a luncheon in Rome, and a moment or two later the grande dame herself passes them by, without cutting them, to be sure, but tactfully avoiding them and walking straight over to a woman who, on inspection, proved to be the beautiful Newport divorcee of highest fashion who had repelled Mrs. Detrimental's every advance at self-introduction aboard the North German Lloyd steamer coming over. She was actually comparing notes with their new-made Roman acquaintance and staring dubiously !

There was a North American chill in the air of the Ritz, and our heroine, with her daughter and *avant courier*, the secretary, was relieved enough to be driven up the Champs Elysee to the Elysee Palais Hotel for a cup of tea. About half an hour after their arrival, their whilom Roman acquaintance was ushered in, accompanied by a little group of ultra-fashionable folk. Mrs. Detrimental stepped forward and greeted her with effusion, but her " friend," while not manifesting actual displeasure, drew her aside and presented her, not to the smart people with whom she was talking, but to a Mrs. Van and Miss Van ———, old friends of her mother's, from New York. Mrs. Detrimental's spirits rose at the sound of the name indicative of one of the oldest families of the metropolis, but the secretary, by a course of delicate but adroit questioning, repressed that comfortable emotion. The Van ———s did not belong to the fashionable branch of their family and did not even know the Gallatins, the Frederic J. de Peysters, the Alexander Van Rensselaers, the Frederic H. Bettses or, in fact, any of the group of New York's old patrician families nearest the throne of the smart set.

The two women were able to find partial relief for their emotions of vexation by cutting dead as a door nail two of their " detrimental " friends of the upper West Side, New York, contingent who suddenly arrived upon the scene of discomfiture. But almost in the next carriage passed some Californians who knew all about them and were voluble talkers, too. At the Ambassador's, to cap the climax, Mrs. Detrimental met with a rebuff from headquarters. It seems that two weeks later the President of France was to give a ball at the Elysee Palace and our heroine, in the momentary absence of her secretary, ventured to ask the Ambassador to secure three invitations for her, bolstering up her claims with the avowal that her family came over with William the Conqueror and was of the purest Norman blood.

"My good Madame, isn't it sufficient for any family in the United States to have started in all right with its own country?" the Ambassador replied, tartly.

Safe in the seclusion of their carriage, the secretary delivers himself: "Pardon my plainness of speech, Madame, but that's what I'm hired for. Don't, I beg of you, ever trust yourself to talk on 'family' again to your dying day. It is only bundling out the old livery stable in Denver, your miners'-cook of a grandmother and every other ridiculous scrap of family history which you implored me to be on my guard against exposing. The very notice of our arrival, with the fulsome mention of the social attentions which we received in Rome, which

I had inserted in the Paris edition of the New York *Herald* just to humor you, is working mischief. Certain of those society people from the Grand Hotel there, are this very moment in Paris and they are beginning to analyze, and I'm afraid they will never stop analyzing. The odds are against us in Paris, which is anyhow so overrun with Western people from the States that it seems like another Chicago. We must beat a retreat to London."

THE SHOWER OF GOLD IN LONDON.

In London, Mrs. Detrimental and her suite put up at Claridge's. In Paris they had received the cold shoulder, but had acquired experience. In London, however, the secretary managed to get them speedily presented to Lord and Lady Down-in-the-Heel, nobility of exalted station but crumbling fortunes. By an ingenious artifice Lord Down-in-the-Heel was led to manipulate a block of their own mining stock, which brought him in such a yield that he and his titled wife were ready to serve them to the queen's taste, Miss Detrimental being at once thus provided with a chaperon from the peerage. The policy of the Detrimentals was now to avoid their fellow-Americans for a while, until they should ingratiate themselves with the English nobility more thoroughly. They gave several dinners and theatre parties, with titled persons mostly for guests, until finally an American, one of the smartest representatives of Newport's smartest set, asked for an introduction to them at the Italian opera, came and sat in their box and made them promise that they would bring Mr. Detrimental and pay him a three or four days' visit at a fixed date in August at his Newport villa.

The telegraphic cables flashed across the Atlantic to the States the accounts of Mrs. and Miss Detrimental's gowns and gems and of the titled personages who were their guests at the opera. But Mrs. Detrimental was now longing to achieve American triumphs on American soil.

LORD AND LADY DOWN-IN-THE-HEEL.

Mrs. Detrimental was eager to lease Marble House, Newport, for July and August, at the price of a king's ransom, but her secretary and social mentor, whose judgment had all along proven well-nigh infallible, frowned the proposition down in toto. "Do not commit yourself to taking a cottage at Newport until you are sure of your ground, Madame. Go to Newport in a yacht and stop on the yacht."

Mrs. Detrimental urges Lord and Lady Down-in-the-Heel to go over to the States with them, but they both obstinately refuse even to accept an invitation to Newport for August if a yacht should be sent over expressly for them. *Sub rosa* they have heard a thing or two from the States and the Continent, and now that they have got a breach or two in their castle walls repaired and Milady has acquired several changes of raiment which could no longer be termed dowdy, they are starting in to kick over the traces, even in London, for people are beginning to chaff them about "Detrimental" money.

Mrs. Detrimental, nothing daunted, secures as lieutenants for the Newport August campaign two young unmarried noblemen of the British peerage, and her husband hires and puts into commission an elephantine yacht—the largest ever built on American soil. They arrive at the City by the Sea and accept the invitation extended to them in London and now formally renewed for a week-end visit at a villa of the *fin fleur* of the ultra smart set on Ochre Point. Invitations have been sent out for a formal dinner in their honor. The response is cordial and entire.

The dinner passes off joyously, neither Astors nor Vanderbilts present to be sure, but others of the "quality" of almost equal *cachet*. But as soon as the men are left to their post prandial cigars, the women *en masse* turn their backs upon Mrs. and Miss Detrimental, who are left to examine portfolios of water-colors, photographic albums or to study the movements of the heavenly bodies through the open windows.

"Can't you see through it all?—Mr. ——, our host, has some property in Newport he wants to work off on the Detrimentals," one of the smart guests was afterwards overheard whispering in the ladies' dressing-room.

"We are being paid off in our own coin," Miss Detrimental muttered to her mother.

The Detrimentals have received a shouldering of more icy coldness than was ever dealt them in Paris, or even their native habitat. For days afterwards invitations come pouring in for the two noblemen, their guests, but none for the hostesses. Even these members of the British peerage cannot stand the denouement, and beg Mrs. Detrimental to have the yacht pull up anchor for Narragansett Pier, Long Branch, or even Coney Island. In the days of Aunty Paran Stevens' social exploiting, or of the first fancy dress ball given by the Willie K. Vanderbilts, the abstract fact of having two such members of the British peerage as Mrs. Detrimental's guests on one's yacht would have brought half of Newport to terms of capitulation. But times have changed. Certain members of the Newport smart set actually patronize noblemen sometimes nowadays.

Mr. Detrimental, deeply chagrined at his wife's and daughter's defeat in Newport waters two years before, more than half the time in the interim having been passed by them abroad, now ordered a palatial yacht of his own built and again it lies at anchor in Newport harbor. This time Lord and Lady Down-in-the-Heel, who are more hard up than ever before, and have a long visiting list of Newport cottagers, have deigned to be guests of honor on the Detrimental yacht, Milord having in the meanwhile consented to accept some sort of a partnership in the head of the family's mines, and the husband of a pronounced Newport society leader a highly lucrative deal in the stock. A patent medicine cotillon is to be given aboard the yacht, with all sorts of patent nostrums doing little stunts, and with an extraordinary and most sensational vaudeville for a finale, the whole costing thousands of dollars.

The invitations are issued solely by Lord and Lady Down-in-the-Heel, aided somewhat by the smart Newport family who had made money in Mr. Detrimental's mine. The Detrimentals are the guests of their own guests that evening on board of their own yacht.

IN AT THE DEATH.

Fewer than half of the two hundred invitations sent out by Lord and Lady Down-in-the-Heel for the patent medicine cotillon on board the Detrimental yacht were accepted, the fact of Lord Down-in-the-Heel's having come upon a Newport cottager for a loan of a hundred thousand to keep bailiffs and sheriffs at bay on the other side, not tending to swell the number of acceptances for this spectacular fête. Not an Astor, Ogden Mills or Vanderbilt was present, but a goodly number of their friends, especially of the younger set, honored the occasion, thinking the Detrimentals would be "great fun" and there would be plenty of Ruinart.

As for Mrs. Detrimental, the pleasure was never hers of meeting those godesses enshrined in her heart as the chief end of human existence to know—Mrs. Astor, Mrs. John Jacob Astor and Mrs. Cornelius Vanderbilt, Jr., for a social honor of which she little dreamed was in store for her a few days later—she died at *Newport* and was laid away in an ultra-smart grave with a glimpse of Marble House in the dim horizon !

But her daughter, Miss Detrimental, whose life did not go out in fireworks, lived to compel all these social oligarchs to receive her by marrying one of the most courted and powerfully-connected men of the spectacular " 150," having virtually settled a couple of millions upon him by ante-nuptial contract.

FINIS.

THE LEISURE CLASS
IN AMERICA

An Arno Press Collection

Bradley, Hugh. **Such was Saratoga.** 1940

Browne, Junius Henri. **The Great Metropolis:** A Mirror of New York. 1869

Burt, Nathaniel. **The Perennial Philadelphians.** 1963

Canby, Henry Seidel. **Alma Mater:** The Gothic Age of the American College. 1936

Crockett, Albert Stevens. **Peacocks on Parade.** 1931

Croffut, W[illiam] A. **The Vanderbilts.** 1886

Crowninshield, Francis W. **Manners for the Metropolis.** 1909

de Wolfe, Elsie. **The House in Good Taste.** 1913

Ellet, E[lizabeth] F[ries Lummis]. **The Court Circles of the Republic,** or The Beauties and Celebrities of the Nation. 1869

Elliott, Maud Howe. **This Was My Newport.** 1944

Elliott, Maud Howe. **Uncle Sam Ward and His Circle.** 1938

Fairfield, Francis Gerry. **The Clubs of New York** and Croly, [Jane C.] **Sorosis.** 1873/1886. Two vols. in one

[Fawcett, Edgar]. **The Buntling Ball:** A Graeco-American Play. 1885

Fawcett, Edgar. **Social Silhouettes.** 1885

Fiske, Stephen. **Off-Hand Portraits of Prominent New Yorkers.** 1884

Foraker, Julia B. **I Would Live It Again:** Memories of a Vivid Life. 1932

Goodwin, Maud Wilder. **The Colonial Cavalier.** 1895

Hartt, Rollin Lynde. **The People at Play.** 1909

Lehr, Elizabeth Drexel. **"King Lehr" and the Gilded Age.** 1935

Lodge, Henry Cabot. **Early Memories.** 1913

[Longchamp, Ferdinand]. **Asmodeus in New-York.** 1868

McAllister, [Samuel] Ward. **Society as I Have Found It.** 1890

McLean, Evalyn, with Boyden Sparkes. **Father Struck It Rich.** 1936

[Mann, William d'Alton]. **Fads and Fancies of Representative Americans at the Beginning of the Twentieth Century.** 1905

Martin, Frederick Townsend. **The Passing of the Idle Rich.** 1911

Martin, Frederick Townsend. **Things I Remember.** 1913

Maurice, Arthur Bartlett. **Fifth Avenue.** 1918

[Mordecai, Samuel]. **Richmond in By-Gone Days.** 1856

Morris, Lloyd. **Incredible New York.** 1951

Neville, Amelia Ransome. **The Fantastic City:** Memoirs of the Social and Romantic Life of Old San Francisco. 1932

Nichols, Charles Wilbur de Lyon. **The Ultra-Fashionable Peerage of America.** 1904

Pound, Arthur. **The Golden Earth:** The Story of Manhattan's Landed Wealth. 1935

Pulitzer, Ralph. **New York Society on Parade.** 1910

Ripley, Eliza. **Social Life in Old New Orleans.** 1912

Ross, Ishbel. **Silhouette in Diamonds:** The Life of Mrs. Potter Palmer. 1960

Sherwood, M[ary] E[lizabeth W.]. **Manners and Social Usages.** 1897

The Sporting Set. 1975

Van Rensselaer, [May] King. **Newport: Our Social Capital.** 1905

Van Rensselaer, [May] King. **The Social Ladder.** 1924

Wharton, Edith and Ogden Codman, Jr. **The Decoration of Houses.** 1914

Williamson, Jefferson. **The American Hotel.** 1930